OCCASIONAL PAPER 195

The Eastern Caribbean Currency Union
Institutions, Performance, and Policy Issues

Frits van Beek, José Roberto Rosales, Mayra Zermeño,
Ruby Randall, and Jorge Shepherd

INTERNATIONAL MONETARY FUND
Washington DC
July 2000

© 2000 International Monetary Fund

Production: IMF Graphics Section
Typesetting: Alicia Etchebarne-Bourdin
Figures: In-Ok Yoon

Library of Congress Cataloging-in-Publication Data

The Eastern Caribbean Currency Union—institutions, performance, and policy issues / Frits van Beek . . . [et al.].

    p. cm. — (IMF occasional paper ; no. 195)
"July 2000."
ISBN 1-55775-894-8

  1. Eastern Caribbean Currency Union—History. 2. Monetary unions—Caribbean Area—History. 3. Eastern Caribbean Central Bank—History. I. Title: Eastern Caribbean Currency Union. II. Van Beek, Frits. III. Occasional paper (International Monetary Fund); no. 195.

HG742.E27 2000
362.4'9729—dc21

00-039563
CIP

Price: US$20.00
(US$17.50 to full-time faculty members and
students at universities and colleges)

Please send orders to:
International Monetary Fund, Publication Services
700 19th Street, N.W., Washington, D.C. 20431, U.S.A.
Tel.: (202) 623-7430   Telefax: (202) 623-7201
E-mail: publications@imf.org
Internet: http://www.imf.org

recycled paper

Contents

Preface		vii
List of Abbreviations		ix
I	**Overview**	1
II	**The Financial System**	4
	ECCB Institutional Framework	4
	ECCB Monetary Instruments	6
	Financial Institutions	11
	Regulatory Framework	18
III	**Money and Capital Market Development Initiatives**	22
IV	**Recent Economic Developments**	25
	Output, Employment, and Prices	25
	Banana Sector	25
	Tourism	27
	Public Finances	30
	Money and Banking	39
	External Sector	43
V	**Main Regional Policy Issues**	56
	The Currency Union Arrangement	56
	Fiscal Policy	56
	Monetary Issues	58
	External Policy	60
VI	**Conclusions**	63

Boxes

1. Statistical Note	viii
2. Antecedents of the ECCB	5
3. Currency Backing and Limits on Credit to Member Governments	6
4. Prudential Requirements for Commercial Banks	21
5. The EU Banana Regime	31
6. Government Lease-to-Own Liabilities: The Case of Grenada	44
7. Fiscal Reform Objectives and Measures Proposed by the ECCB	57
8. Stabex Grants to the Windward Islands	61

Figure

1. ECCB Area: Exchange Rate Developments, 1981–99	51

Tables

1. ECCB Area: Selected Economic Indicators	2
2. ECCB Area: Allocation of ECCB Credit to Member Governments, 1998/99	7
3. ECCB Area: Detailed Monetary Survey	8
4. ECCB Area: Condensed Balance Sheet and Backing Ratio	9
5. Selected ECCB and International Interest Rates	10
6. ECCB Area: List of Commercial Banks by Territory	12
7. ECCB Area: Weighted Commercial Bank Interest Rates	13
8. ECCB Area: Selected Current and Capital Account Restrictions	14
9. ECCB Area: Output and Population Growth	26
10. ECCB Area: Rate of Growth of Gross Domestic Product by Economic Activity, at Factor Cost, in Constant Prices	27
11. ECCB Area: Contribution of Gross Domestic Product by Economic Activity, at Factor Cost, in Constant Prices	28
12. ECCB Area: Saving and Investment	29
13. ECCB Area: Consumer Prices	29
14. Windward Islands: Selected Banana Sector Indicators	30
15. EU: Duty-Free Banana Import Quotas for ACP Countries	32
16. EU: Comparison of Quota/Tariff Structure Under the Previous and Current Banana Import Regimes	33
17. Windward Islands: Banana Growers Profile	33
18. Windward Islands: Banana Recovery Plan	34
19. Caribbean Region: Stayover Tourist Arrivals	34
20. ECCB Area: Stayover Tourist Arrivals by Country of Origin	35
21. Caribbean Region: Number of Hotel Rooms	35
22. Caribbean Region: Cruise Passenger Arrivals	36
23. Caribbean Region: Visitor Expenditure	36
24. ECCB Area: Selected Public Sector Indicators by Country	37
25. ECCB Area: Public Sector Operations	38
26. ECCB Area: Selected Central Government Indicators by Country	39
27. ECCB Area: Central Government Operations	40
28. ECCB Area: Central Government Expenditure Indicators by Country	41
29. ECCB Area: Central Government Revenue Indicators by Country	42
30. ECCB Area: Average Import Duties and Customs Surcharges	43
31. ECCB Area: Banking System Credit to the Public Sector	45
32. ECCB Area: Public Sector Debt	45
33. ECCB Area: External Arrears	46
34. ECCB Area: Selected Banking System Indicators by Country	47
35. ECCB Area: Sectoral Distribution of Commercial Banks' Loans and Advances	48
36. ECCB Area: Commercial Banks' Overdrafts and Loans by Maturity	49
37. ECCB Area: Selected Monetary Indicators	49
38. ECCB Area: Effective Exchange Rates	50
39. CARICOM: Implementation of Scheduled Reductions in the Maximum Rate of the Common External Tariff	52
40. CARICOM: Common External Tariff Rates	53
41. ECCB Area: Statutory Tax Rates on International Trade and Transactions	53
42. ECCB Area: Summary Balance of Payments	54
43. ECCB Area: Current Account by Country	55

The following symbols have been used throughout this paper:

. . .   to indicate that data are not available;

—   to indicate that the figure is zero or less than half the final digit shown, or that the item does not exist;

–   between years or months (e.g., 1998–99 or January–June) to indicate the years or months covered, including the beginning and ending years or months;

/   between years (e.g., 1998/99) to indicate a fiscal (financial) year.

"Billion" means a thousand million.

Minor discrepancies between constituent figures and totals are due to rounding.

The term "country," as used in this paper, does not in all cases refer to a territorial entity that is a state as understood by international law and practice; the term also covers some territorial entities that are not states, but for which statistical data are maintained and provided internationally on a separate and independent basis.

Preface

IMF staff teams visited Basseterre, St. Kitts and Nevis, during November 23–27, 1998 and February 22–25, 1999 to hold policy discussions with senior officials of the Eastern Caribbean Central Bank (ECCB). The ECCB representatives were headed by Governor K. Dwight Venner. The discussions focused on a review of recent performance and on key regional policy issues in the monetary and banking, fiscal, external, and other areas.

These visits provided a framework to complement the bilateral surveillance discussions held in 1998–99 with the ECCB member countries that are also members of the IMF. Given the widening range of economic policies formulated and implemented at the regional level, and in view of the special characteristics of the ECCB area, both the IMF and regional authorities believe that regional discussions should be held more frequently. Accordingly, as part of a move to a more formal and comprehensive dialogue with the Eastern Caribbean regional institutions, reports on such discussions will be presented to the IMF's Executive Board on a regular basis.

The material presented in this paper was originally prepared for discussion in the IMF Executive Board in March 1999; it is based on data through December 1998, but takes account also of key developments in 1999. The paper includes a large amount of statistical information that is not readily available elsewhere in a single source (see Box 1). The authors are grateful to the management and staff of the Eastern Caribbean Central Bank for extensive discussions and comments and for their assistance in providing data and other source material, and to colleagues in the IMF for helpful comments on previous drafts.

The authors wish to express their appreciation to Jeremy Clift of the External Relations Department for editing the paper and coordinating its publication. They are also grateful for the assistance provided by Patricia Parsons and Alfred Go of the Western Hemisphere Department in processing the original text, tables, and other materials. The views expressed are the sole responsibility of the authors and do not necessarily reflect those of the IMF staff or Executive Board, or the Eastern Caribbean Central Bank.

PREFACE

Box 1. Statistical Note

The banking, balance of payments, debt, and national accounts data presented in this paper were provided by the Eastern Caribbean Central Bank (ECCB). Discrepancies with figures presented in recent IMF reports on the six independent member states of the ECCB are due largely to differences in timeliness (ECCB data are updated as of December 1999) and, to a lesser extent, to differences in compilation methodologies and sources. Despite steady convergence in recent years, differences remain between ECCB and the IMF country desk data on the balance payments and external debt of certain countries. The data presented on public sector revenue, expenditure, and financing are from the IMF data files maintained for the six independent member states of the ECCB, and any differences with data shown in recent IMF Staff Country Reports are due to updating of preliminary data and earlier projections for 1997 and 1998.

As regards regional coverage, the national accounts and other data presented in Tables 1, 9–13, and 19–23 generally exclude Anguilla and Montserrat, except for regional GDP and tourism, as indicated in the footnotes. The fiscal data shown in Tables 24–33 exclude Anguilla and Montserrat, while the monetary data (Tables 2–7 and 34–37) and the balance of payments data (Tables 42–43) include those two territories.

These differences in sources and country coverage preclude a high degree of intersectoral consistency. While the monetary and balance of payments data are fully consistent, this is not the case for the fiscal and balance of payments data. It may be noted that the combined balance of payments for the region does not net out intraregional transactions for lack of the requisite detail, except for intraregional capital flows identified in the accounts of the commercial banks. Furthermore, the overall balance of payments of the region does not equal the sum of the imputed overall payments balances of the eight individual countries.

List of Abbreviations

ACP	African, Caribbean, and Pacific countries
BCCB	British Caribbean Currency Board
CARICOM	Caribbean Community and Common Market
CDB	Caribbean Development Bank
CET	Common External Tariff (of CARICOM)
CMCF	Caribbean Multilateral Clearing Facility
ECCA	Eastern Caribbean Currency Authority
ECCB	Eastern Caribbean Central Bank
ECCM	Eastern Caribbean Common Market
ECCSD	Eastern Caribbean Central Securities Depository
ECCSR	Eastern Caribbean Central Securities Registry
ECCU	Eastern Caribbean Currency Union
ECEF	Eastern Caribbean Enterprise Fund
ECGS	Export Credit Guarantee Scheme
ECHMB	Eastern Caribbean Home Mortgage Bank
ECSE	Eastern Caribbean Securities Exchange
ECSRC	Eastern Caribbean Securities Regulatory Commission
ECUTC	Eastern Caribbean Unit Trust Company
EU	European Union
GATT	General Agreement on Tariffs and Trade
NAFTA	North American Free Trade Agreement
OECS	Organization of Eastern Caribbean States
RGSM	Regional Government Securities Market
UBA	Uniform Banking Act
WBDECO	The Windward Islands Banana Development and Export Company
WTO	The World Trade Organization

I Overview

Eastern Caribbean countries institutionalized political and economic cooperation through the establishment of the Organization of Eastern Caribbean States (OECS) with the Treaty of Basseterre in 1981. Two years later they set up the Eastern Caribbean Central Bank (ECCB), which replaced the Eastern Caribbean Currency Authority. The eight member countries and territories of the ECCB are Antigua and Barbuda, Dominica, Grenada, St. Kitts and Nevis, St. Lucia, and St. Vincent and the Grenadines, which are independent states and members of the IMF, and Anguilla and Montserrat, which are territories of the United Kingdom.[1] The six independent OECS states and Montserrat are also members of the Caribbean Common Market, CARICOM, established in 1973.

The OECS members share a common currency, the Eastern Caribbean dollar, which has been pegged to the U.S. dollar since 1976 at EC$2.70=US$1, and was pegged to the British pound at EC$4.80=£1 from 1950 to 1976. Prior to the recent inception of the European Central Bank, the ECCB was one of only three common central banks in the world and the only one where the member countries have pooled all their foreign reserves, the convertibility of the common currency is fully self-supported, and the parity of the exchange rate has not been changed.

This occasional paper reviews recent developments, policy issues, and institutional arrangements in the member countries of the Eastern Caribbean Currency Union (ECCU), and looks at the ECCB's institutional arrangements, the financial system and its supervision, and the central bank's initiatives to establish a single financial space.

Two aspects of the ECCU economies stand out—their very small size and their vulnerability to shocks. Geographic barriers complicate the functioning of a single market, and even taken as a whole, the ECCU is a very small economy. The total population is approximately half a million and combined gross domestic product (GDP) was estimated at US$2.6 billion in 1998, or about $4,500 per capita, which is relatively high in the Caribbean. Per capita GDP varies from a high of nearly US$9,000 for Antigua and Barbuda to a low of about $2,800 for St. Vincent and the Grenadines (Table 1). Indivisibilities and high unit costs are barriers to many forms of economic activity: the market is so small that importing is sometimes unprofitable, and production even more so. The independent states range in size from St. Kitts and Nevis, with 269 sq. km., to Dominica, with 750 sq. km., and populations range from 41,000 in St. Kitts and Nevis to 140,000 in St. Lucia (Anguilla and Montserrat are even smaller). The OECS economies are exposed to natural disasters—particularly hurricanes, and less frequently drought and volcanic eruption. Because of their small size, the impact of a natural disaster can be far more devastating than for a larger economy where the damage is localized.[2]

Until the 1950s, the Eastern Caribbean countries were overwhelmingly agricultural—mainly specializing in either bananas or sugar. There has since been a steady shift, accelerating in the 1980s, away from agriculture and toward tourism. In general, the countries in which income has risen most are those where this shift has proceeded the furthest. Overall, tourism today accounts for 10 percent of GDP and agriculture 8 percent. Manufacturing remains relatively small (less than 6 percent) and consists largely of food processing and enclave industries such as garments and small assembly plants. Construction is significant (around 10½ percent), much of it serving the needs of tourism.

The economies in the region are very open: merchandise imports averaged 53 percent of GDP during 1990–98; merchandise exports 16½ percent of GDP; and the surplus in the nonfactor services balance, 24 percent of GDP. Also, the sum of current and capital transfers has been very large, averaging close to 8

---

[1] Anguilla did not join the ECCB until 1987. The British Virgin Islands are an associate member of the OECS, but not of the ECCB.

[2] For a discussion of vulnerability and other aspects of the economies of small states, see *Small States: Meeting Challenges in the Global Economy*, Report of the Commonwealth Secretariat/World Bank Joint Task Force on Small States, April 2000.

I OVERVIEW

Table 1. ECCB Area: Selected Economic Indicators[1]

	1990	1991	1992	1993	1994	1995	1996	1997	1998
	(Annual percentage change)								
Real GDP at factor cost[2]	4.7	0.7	3.9	2.6	3.0	0.7	2.7	3.1	2.3
Real per capita GDP[2]	3.7	1.4	2.5	0.9	1.9	0.0	2.8	2.7	2.9
Export volume	−0.4	−11.8	8.7	−6.0	−10.4	6.6	−5.4	−6.2	10.9
Import volume	0.8	0.1	−4.5	8.8	−3.5	−2.2	5.7	14.7	4.8
Terms of trade	n.a.	1.9	−3.1	−1.0	1.2	−3.9	−3.1	3.7	4.6
Consumer prices (end of period)	5.1	4.3	3.6	2.5	2.2	2.1	2.1	2.6	3.1
	(Percent of GDP)								
Overall fiscal balance	−2.4	−2.5	−1.1	−0.7	−2.0	−0.6	−0.6	−3.8	−2.8
Government tax revenue	21.5	21.1	20.9	21.4	21.1	21.4	21.5	21.4	21.3
External current account balance[2]	−16.9	−16.6	−10.6	−10.7	−11.0	−9.7	−14.4	−16.0	−15.8
Gross national saving[3]	16.7	14.2	16.7	18.8	17.8	22.2	17.5	15.9	15.3
Public saving	3.6	3.8	4.0	4.7	4.0	4.0	4.0	3.3	3.8
Private saving	13.1	10.4	12.7	14.1	13.8	18.1	13.5	12.6	11.6
Gross domestic investment	33.6	30.8	27.3	29.4	28.8	31.9	31.9	32.0	31.2
Public investment	8.7	9.1	7.0	8.0	8.4	7.2	7.3	4.3	9.6
Private investment	24.9	21.7	20.3	21.4	20.4	24.7	24.6	22.7	21.6
Gross foreign assets, ECCB	12.0	12.4	14.6	13.5	12.3	14.2	12.6	12.6	13.7
Public external debt (end of period)[4]	42.6	49.8	49.2	48.4	49.3	50.5	47.9	45.7	45.1
	(U.S. dollars)								
Per capita GDP	3,145	3,312	3,508	3,592	3,789	3,882	4,087	4,291	4,538
Anguilla	6,262	6,200	6,548	6,911	7,471	7,280	7,429	7,450	7,631
Antigua and Barbuda	6,139	6,425	6,551	6,959	7,530	7,301	7,876	8,459	8,976
Dominica	2,328	2,535	2,679	2,750	2,912	2,995	3,184	3,229	3,376
Grenada	2,334	2,527	2,600	2,578	2,685	2,805	2,979	3,165	3,348
Montserrat	5,652	5,117	5,390	5,907	6,118	5,673	6,186	10,754	10,822
St. Kitts and Nevis	3,802	4,013	4,261	4,557	5,151	5,298	5,812	6,502	6,814
St. Lucia	3,103	3,293	3,601	3,555	3,634	3,815	3,869	3,876	4,138
St. Vincent and the Grenadines	1,872	1,995	2,172	2,183	2,214	2,387	2,504	2,631	2,810
Memorandum items:									
Total GDP of the region, at market prices (US$ m)[2]	1,674	1,769	1,898	1,970	2,099	2,176	2,295	2,415	2,579
Total population of the region (thousands of inhabitants)[2]	532	534	541	548	554	561	562	563	568

Sources: Eastern Caribbean Central Bank, and IMF staff estimates.
[1] The area includes Antigua and Barbuda, Dominica, Grenada, St. Kitts and Nevis, St. Lucia, and St. Vincent and the Grenadines; except otherwise indicated.
[2] Also includes Anguilla and Montserrat.
[3] Defined as the gross domestic investment plus the external current account balance.
[4] Includes external arrears.

percent of GDP over the same period. Foreign direct investment (over 9 percent of GDP) and loans to the public sector help cover the current account deficit. Most of the region's trade is with the United States and the European Union, both of which grant trade preferences; Japan and other Caribbean countries are also important trading partners.

Despite difficult fundamentals, economic performance in the region was strong in the late 1970s and 1980s and has remained broadly satisfactory in the 1990s. Real GDP growth averaged 6 percent a year during 1977–89, but slowed to an average of 2½ percent a year during 1990–98; partial information suggests that real GDP grew by around 3 percent in 1999. Given the openness of the economies and the exchange rate peg, inflation has been in line with that in the major trading partners, averaging about 3 percent a year during 1990–98; in 1999, inflation was less than 2 percent. This outcome was facilitated by the "strong EC dollar policy" pursued by the ECCB and the generally sound fiscal policies followed by most countries.

In the course of the 1990s, however, the slowdown in growth was accompanied by a weakening of the fiscal positions in several countries, and the medium-term outlook has changed. The availability of concessional foreign financing has been declining, as some countries have "graduated" and donors have shifted priorities; the European Union's (EU) banana regime is being opened to competition; sugar production, even for export to the protected markets,[3] is of questionable viability; and there are indications that the light manufacturing sector is losing ground to lower wage areas.[4]

On the brighter side, the region has seen a marked increase in tourist arrivals in recent years. At the same time, some diversification is taking place, with moderate growth in nontraditional agriculture and the emergence of firms involved in data processing and informatics, and in offshore financial and gaming services.

---

[3]St. Kitts and Nevis produces some 20,000 tons of sugar a year for export under quotas to the United States and the European Union. The state-owned sugar company incurs a loss of some EC$18 million a year.

[4]There is some evidence that firms have left the region for Mexico to benefit from the NAFTA arrangement.

II The Financial System

ECCB Institutional Framework

The establishment of the *Eastern Caribbean Central Bank (ECCB)* in 1983 was the culmination of a long period of monetary cooperation dating back to 1950 when the British Caribbean Currency Board (BCCB) was created (Box 2). The BCCB, which functioned as a currency board proper and maintained a foreign exchange cover of 100 percent of the currency issue, was replaced by the Eastern Caribbean Currency Authority (ECCA) in 1965, when the Eastern Caribbean dollar (EC$) was introduced and pegged to the pound sterling at a rate of EC$4.80 = £1. Under the ECCA, the foreign exchange backing was set at 70 percent and then reduced to 60 percent in 1975. Following a series of depreciations of the pound, the Eastern Caribbean dollar was pegged to the U.S. dollar in July 1976 at the then prevailing market cross-rate of EC$2.70 per U.S. dollar. The parity has remained fixed at that level.

Like the ECCA and the BCCB before it, the ECCB has the sole right to issue the common currency, and the member countries surrender their foreign exchange to the common reserves pool administered by the ECCB. Each country, however, has unrestricted access to the common reserve pool as long as it has the domestic currency to make it effective.[5] All ECCB bank notes are coded according to the country to which they are issued. This enables the ECCB to allocate profits to the member governments taking into account the currency issued in each territory and to calculate *imputed* reserves for each as the sum of currency in circulation and its net claims on the government and the commercial banks in each territory.[6]

The ECCB is governed by two separate bodies: the *Monetary Council* and the *Board of Directors*. The *Monetary Council* consists of eight members, one minister appointed by each member state (each with one vote), and is the highest decision-making authority of the ECCB. The chairmanship of the Council is rotated every year. The Monetary Council meets three times a year and is responsible for providing policy guidance to management. The *Board of Directors* has ten members, including the Governor (who is the Chairman), the Deputy Governor, and one Director appointed by each participating government. It meets five times a year and is responsible for the general operations of the Bank, regional and international economic relations, and coordination of plans and programs. The Governor and Deputy Governor are appointed by the Monetary Council, normally for five-year terms, and can be reappointed.

A major reason for the creation of the ECCB was that member states wanted a central bank capable of playing a more active role in promoting the region's development. Consequently, the objectives of the ECCB as stated in its charter are the regulation of money and credit; the maintenance of monetary stability; the promotion of credit and exchange conditions and a sound financial structure conducive to regional growth and development; and promotion of economic development of the member states. In practice, the principal objective of the ECCB's monetary policy, and the primary benefit of the currency union, has been sustaining credibility of the fixed exchange rate regime, which has been central to the region's price stability. Macroeconomic stability has in turn facilitated economic growth. Other clear economic benefits that member countries have derived from the currency union include risk-pooling through

---

[5]In this sense, an individual ECCB member country cannot have a "balance of payments problem," only a fiscal problem. Accordingly, external arrears by an ECCB member country that is also a member of the IMF are not considered evidence of an exchange restriction under Article VIII, Section 2(a) of the IMF's Articles of Agreement.

[6]These imputed reserves are *not* a measure of the foreign reserves at a member country's disposal. For one thing, the sum of countries' imputed gross reserves falls considerably short of the total foreign assets of the ECCB. Another difficulty is that the coded notes travel freely from one country to another, creating a wedge between currency issued and currency in circulation in each country. Nevertheless, changes in the imputed reserves (together with changes in the typically small amounts of SDRs and other foreign assets held by individual governments) are used to estimate the balance of payments of the individual countries as compiled by the ECCB and the IMF. The sum of these "imputed" balance of payments of the individual countries does not equal the overall balance of payments of the currency union, after adjustment for intraregional transactions.

> **Box 2. Antecedents of the ECCB**
>
> The antecedents of the ECCB date back to the development of the currency arrangements for the British colonial territories in the Caribbean. In the early days, notes issued by the foreign commercial banks operating in the region and coins issued by the United Kingdom were circulating concurrently. Starting in the 1920s, currency was also issued by three different Boards of Commissioners of Currency, in Trinidad and Tobago, British Guyana, and Barbados (which also served the Leeward and Windward Islands).[1] At the West Indian Currency Conference in 1946, these countries agreed to establish a unified decimal currency system based on the West Indian dollar, and in 1950 they created the British Caribbean Currency Board (BCCB). The BCCB was given the sole right to issue notes and coins, and the mandate of keeping full foreign exchange cover to ensure convertibility at the exchange parity of 4.8 West Indian dollars for one pound sterling. Trinidad and Tobago withdrew from the BCCB upon independence in 1962 and established its own central bank. British Guyana did the same in early 1965.
>
> The BCCB was replaced by the Eastern Caribbean Currency Authority (ECCA) in January 1965, the original members of which were Barbados, the Leeward Islands, and the Windward Islands except Grenada,[2] which joined in 1968. The West Indian dollar was replaced by the Eastern Caribbean dollar with the same exchange parity. The foreign exchange cover was set initially at 70 percent. The Authority served as an advisor, banker, and fiscal agent to member governments and compiled financial and economic data on the members. Through the Clearing Agreement, the Authority provided commercial banks operating in the area with a facility for clearing interbank indebtedness. Banks also made use of a facility for surrendering foreign currency in exchange for interest-bearing deposit accounts.
>
> Following the devaluation of the pound sterling in 1967, Barbados proposed that the Currency Agreement be amended to allow the ECCA to change the parity of the Eastern Caribbean dollar in the event of a devaluation of the pound. Such an amendment was never made, and in 1972, after the floating of the pound, Barbados established its own central bank. Following the withdrawal of Barbados, the ECCA's headquarters was moved to St. Kitts. The foreign exchange cover was reduced to 60 percent in 1975. The ECCA shifted the link of the Eastern Caribbean dollar from the pound to the U.S. dollar in 1976. At the same time, there was an attempt to improve bank regulation by gathering information on commercial banks on a regular basis. The ECCA also assumed a broader role; for example, in 1977 it became a cosignatory for establishing the Multilateral Clearing Facility in the Caribbean Community and Common Market (CARICOM) replacing the existing bilateral clearing arrangement. The process of regional integration took another step forward with the creation of the ECCB in 1983.[3]
>
> ---
>
> [1] The Leeward Islands comprise Anguilla, Antigua and Barbuda, Montserrat, and St. Kitts and Nevis; the Windward Islands are Dominica, Grenada, St. Lucia, and St. Vincent and the Grenadines.
>
> [2] Grenada initially formed a political union with Trinidad and Tobago and used its currency as legal tender until it joined the ECCA in November 1968.
>
> [3] Regional cooperation in other areas included the creation of the Caribbean Free Trade Agreement (CFTA) in 1967 by Antigua and Barbuda, Barbados, Trinidad and Tobago, and Guyana, joined in 1968 by the Windward Islands, St. Kitts and Nevis, and Montserrat. The Leeward and Windward Islands formed the East Caribbean Common Market (ECCM) in 1968. CARICOM was established in 1973, superseding the CFTA. The Organization of East Caribbean States was established in 1981, superseding the ECCM.

a common foreign exchange reserve pool,[7] and the achievement of economies of scale in central bank operations through the spread of overhead costs.

Stability of the Eastern Caribbean dollar is maintained through strong foreign currency backing, as the Bank is bound by its Articles of Agreement to maintain the level of pooled reserves at not less than 60 percent of its demand liabilities.[8] This implies a limit on domestic assets of 40 percent of Eastern Caribbean dollar-denominated demand liabilities. The Articles of Agreement stipulate that the ECCB may, at its discretion, extend credit to member governments under a number of specified lines, but subject to prescribed limits (Box 3). The sum of the maximum amounts the ECCB could lend under these credit lines, including the outstanding balances on the "special deposit" loans,[9] typically exceeds the 40 percent global limit on domestic assets.

---

[7] Reserve pooling smoothes differences in the timing of inflows into the reserve pool arising from the different composition of member countries' exports.

[8] Namely, reserve money, consisting of bank reserves and currency issued. The backing ratio is calculated as external assets less commercial bank foreign currency deposits with the ECCB, divided by demand liabilities.

[9] Prior to the creation of the ECCB, some participating governments required commercial banks to maintain "special deposits"—in lieu of reserve requirements—which were never refunded. This outstanding liability of member governments was credited to the statutory reserve accounts of the commercial banks, while the ECCB assumed the governments' liabilities in this regard.

II THE FINANCIAL SYSTEM

Box 3. Currency Backing and Limits on Credit to Member Governments

Stability in the value of the Eastern Caribbean dollar is maintained through strong foreign currency backing, as the Bank is bound by its Articles of Agreement to maintain, at all times, the level of pooled official reserves at no less than 60 percent of the value of its demand liabilities. This implies a **global limit on domestic assets** of 40 percent of demand liabilities, which the Bank then distributes to participating governments, over a range of credit categories. In practice, the ECCB has typically maintained a foreign exchange backing ratio in excess of 95 percent.

According to its Articles of Agreement, the ECCB is permitted to provide credit to member governments in the form of: (i) temporary advances; (ii) holdings of member state treasury bills; (iii) holdings of securities other than treasury bills; (iv) holdings of corporate bonds issued by corporations established under the authority of any participating government; and (v) the assumption of participating government "special deposit liabilities" to financial institutions.

The amounts of such lending are subject to the following rules:

- *Temporary advances* to participating governments are intended for assisting with seasonal credit needs, and are limited to 5 percent of participating governments' average annual recurrent revenue over the three preceding financial years. Such advances must be amortized over a period of no more than 12 months, and are debited from governments' operating accounts.
- ECCB holdings of *treasury bills* of participating governments that mature within 91 days of the date of their acquisition by the Bank must not exceed 10 percent of the estimated recurrent revenue of that government for that current year (based on the approved budget for the current financial year).
- ECCB holdings of government securities maturing in no more than 15 years from the date of acquisition by the Bank must not exceed 15 percent of the currency issued and in circulation and other demand liabilities. In practice, the Bank bases this calculation on the average currency in circulation and other demand liabilities over the preceding 12 months, owing to seasonal variations and the varying deposit behavior of the commercial banks.
- ECCB holdings of corporate bonds, which must mature within ten years from the date of acquisition by the Bank, are limited to 2½ percent of the average annual government revenue over the preceding three financial years.
- The ECCB continues to service participating governments' "special deposit" loans; the original amount assumed by the Bank was EC$75.7 million, and as of end-1998 this loan balance was EC$30.8 million.

Because the sum of the amounts calculated for these different credit categories usually exceeds the global credit ceiling, and because the Bank must also make provisions for its responsibility as the "lender of last resort" to the banking system, actual credit allocations, by type of individual credit category, are based on each member government's share of total regional recurrent revenue. These individual country limits serve only as lending guidelines.

The Agreement authorizes the Bank to make secured advances to banks, but it does not specify the terms of the ECCB's involvement as a "lender of last resort" in the event of bank crises.

At the beginning of each financial year (April 1), the ECCB's monetary program allocates the global limit (calculated conservatively in relation to the monthly average of the monetary liabilities of the previous year) to the member governments in proportion to each government's share of total regional recurrent revenue. The actual credit available to each government for the financial year is the amount of the allocation less all outstanding balances and arrears (Table 2). In practice, net new lending to governments has been minimal and on balance, the stock of outstanding credit declined during 1990–98 (Table 3), as member governments have been reluctant to borrow and the ECCB has been conservative in its allocation of credit, typically maintaining a foreign exchange backing ratio in excess of 95 percent (Table 4). In this way, the ECCB has room to exercise its responsibilities as "lender of last resort" to the banking system when necessary, and to lend to governments during natural disasters or other pressing circumstances.[10]

ECCB Monetary Instruments

The ECCB's Articles of Agreement authorize the Bank to use discount rates and rediscount rates, establish differential rates and ceilings for various classes of transactions, determine priority areas for credit distribution in cooperation with member governments, and establish a schedule of reserve re-

---

[10]Instances where the backing ratio dipped well below the "golden rule" typically reflect such emergency lending to governments. For example, in the early 1980s the backing ratio was down below 80 percent, following the eruption of the volcano in St. Vincent and the Grenadines in 1979 and the 1980–81 hurricanes that damaged Dominica and St. Lucia.

Table 2. ECCB Area: Allocation of ECCB Credit to Member Governments 1998/99[1]

(Millions of Eastern Caribbean dollars, unless otherwise indicated)

Territory	Est. Recurrent Revenue (1)	Percent of Total Recurrent Revenue (2)	Credit Allocation (Share of Fiduciary) (3)	Treasury Bills and Advances					Debentures			Special Deposits (11)	Arrears (12)	Total Available (13)
				Allocation (4)	Holdings (5)	Advances and Operational Balances (6)	Balance (7)	Allocation (8)	Holdings (9)	Balance (10)				
Anguilla	57	3.1	9.6	6.0	0.0	0.0	6.0	3.6	0.0	3.6	0.0	0.0	9.6
Antigua and Barbuda	392	21.2	66.0	41.3	15.9	2.2	23.2	24.8	14.8	10.0	8.7	4.1	20.3
Dominica	195	10.5	32.8	20.5	12.7	2.0	5.8	12.3	6.5	5.8	2.7	0.3	8.6
Grenada	247	13.3	41.6	26.0	13.7	0.0	12.3	15.6	6.6	9.0	8.3	1.8	11.2
Montserrat	16	0.9	2.7	1.7	0.0	0.0	1.7	1.0	1.8	−0.8	0.0	0.0	0.9
St. Kitts and Nevis	265	14.3	44.6	27.9	5.7	0.0	22.2	16.7	0.0	16.7	3.1	0.0	35.8
St. Lucia	439	23.7	73.9	46.2	19.1	1.5	25.6	27.7	5.0	22.7	6.5	0.0	41.8
St. Vincent and the Grenadines	242	13.1	40.7	25.5	0.0	0.3	25.2	15.3	6.9	8.4	3.0	0.0	30.6
Total	1,853	100.0	312.0	195.0	67.1	6.0	122.0	117.0	41.6	75.4	32.3	6.3	158.8

Source: Eastern Caribbean Central Bank.

[1] Financial year April-March. Outstanding balances in columns (3) through (13) are as of March 31, 1998.

Note: The total credit allocation or "fiduciary" (3), equal to 40 percent of average demand liabilities in 1997/98, is distributed in proportion to total recurrent revenue (1). The allocation of treasury bills is calculated separately and subtracted from (3) to yield the allocation of debentures (8). Total available credit (13) is the sum of the available balances of treasury bills (7) and debentures (10) less special deposits (11) and arrears (12).

II THE FINANCIAL SYSTEM

Table 3. ECCB Area: Detailed Monetary Survey[1]
(Millions of Eastern Caribbean dollars)

	December 31								
	1990	1991	1992	1993	1994	1995	1996	1997	1998
Net foreign assets	639.0	703.5	761.7	725.2	705.3	929.4	696.5	653.4	990.8
Central bank	530.2	562.8	718.7	707.0	685.4	818.2	758.8	815.8	953.2
Foreign assets	543.8	590.1	746.6	719.5	698.1	836.3	778.7	823.7	957.5
Foreign liabilities	13.7	27.3	28.0	12.5	12.8	18.1	19.9	7.9	4.3
Commercial banks	108.8	140.6	43.1	18.2	19.9	111.2	−62.3	−162.3	37.6
Foreign assets	548.4	587.6	623.1	665.8	730.8	822.8	843.7	867.1	1,086.9
Foreign liabilities	439.6	446.9	580.0	647.5	710.9	711.6	905.9	1,029.4	1,049.3
Net domestic assets	1,810.6	1,959.4	2,106.4	2,420.2	2,687.2	2,942.4	3,249.4	3,669.4	3,871.2
Domestic credit	2,169.2	2,387.3	2,567.0	2,891.0	2,992.3	3,299.8	3,651.8	4,135.6	4,434.0
Private sector	2,210.3	2,447.0	2,733.4	3,051.8	3,171.1	3,498.1	3,923.8	4,443.9	4,799.0
Households	1,162.9	1,257.6	1,386.2	1,558.4	1,609.2	1,757.3	1,985.3	2,385.2	2,587.8
Businesses									
Credit	1,047.4	1,189.4	1,347.2	1,493.3	1,561.9	1,740.8	1,938.5	2,058.7	2,213.9
Loans	1,045.5	1,187.3	1,345.3	1,490.9	1,558.6	1,735.4	1,936.0	2,056.5	2,211.5
Investments	1.8	2.1	1.9	2.5	3.3	5.5	2.4	2.2	2.4
Nonbank financial institutions (net)	−104.9	−110.4	−155.2	−166.8	−127.0	−166.5	−198.9	−189.9	−198.2
Credit	38.7	40.7	21.7	18.5	41.4	30.6	48.1	51.0	59.5
Loans	25.8	25.8	16.6	12.7	41.0	25.3	28.3	29.4	30.9
Investments	13.0	14.9	5.1	5.8	0.4	5.3	19.8	21.5	28.7
Deposits	143.6	151.1	176.9	185.3	168.4	197.1	247.0	240.9	257.8
Subsidiaries and affiliates (net)	0.0	0.0	0.0	0.0	−9.0	−19.6	−52.8	−68.3	−55.6
Credit	0.0	0.0	0.0	0.0	9.5	13.1	19.1	21.2	36.0
Loans	0.0	0.0	0.0	0.0	0.3	2.5	6.2	6.2	21.4
Investments	0.0	0.0	0.0	0.0	9.3	10.6	12.9	15.0	14.7
Deposits	0.0	0.0	0.0	0.0	18.5	32.7	71.9	89.6	91.6
Nonfinancial public enterprises (net)[2]	−293.7	−327.6	−332.1	−341.0	−383.1	−424.8	−474.2	−502.7	−570.9
Credit	114.0	111.1	141.3	166.0	207.7	257.4	272.7	282.2	311.5
Loans	114.0	110.4	141.3	166.0	207.7	257.0	272.3	279.6	303.9
Investments	0.0	0.7	0.0	0.0	0.0	0.4	0.4	2.7	7.6
Deposits	407.7	438.7	473.4	507.0	590.8	682.2	746.9	785.0	882.4
Central government (net)	358.0	378.3	320.9	347.1	340.3	412.5	453.8	452.7	459.0
Credit	462.7	483.6	472.8	497.3	501.3	605.2	654.3	692.2	822.0
Central bank	169.9	172.4	127.7	122.7	116.5	105.5	109.1	95.3	89.2
Advances	13.6	20.4	13.0	4.1	8.1	11.6	7.7	3.3	2.0
Operating accounts	0.0	0.0	4.7	3.5	5.8	0.6	2.7	1.8	4.3
Loans	73.5	67.7	66.6	62.2	59.1	48.1	42.7	36.9	30.8
Treasury bills	48.8	50.3	11.0	15.2	10.0	7.1	13.0	10.1	10.1
Debentures	34.0	34.0	32.4	37.7	33.4	36.5	41.5	41.5	40.7
Interest due on securities	0.0	0.0	0.0	0.0	0.0	1.7	1.5	1.8	1.4
Commercial banks	292.7	311.2	345.1	374.6	384.8	499.6	545.2	596.9	732.6
Loans and advances	196.8	221.9	212.4	225.4	238.0	348.2	380.7	426.4	564.9
Treasury bills	33.6	31.8	59.0	75.8	67.8	74.1	86.2	92.5	86.2
Debentures	62.4	57.4	73.6	73.4	79.1	77.3	78.3	78.0	81.5
Deposits	104.7	105.4	151.8	150.2	161.0	192.6	200.5	239.5	363.0
Central bank	14.8	14.5	10.7	7.2	10.0	18.3	16.5	17.6	31.3
Deposits	8.3	9.7	3.9	6.0	6.1	10.3	9.7	13.5	24.0
Sinking fund call account	6.5	4.7	6.8	0.6	2.5	5.3	5.4	2.5	6.1
Operating accounts	0.0	0.0	0.1	0.7	1.5	2.8	1.3	1.7	1.3
Commercial banks	89.9	90.9	141.1	142.9	151.0	174.4	184.1	221.9	331.6
Other items (net)	−359.1	−427.9	−460.6	−470.8	−304.9	−357.4	−402.4	−466.3	−563.0
Monetary liabilities (M2)	2,449.6	2,662.9	2,868.2	3,145.4	3,392.7	3,871.8	3,945.9	4,322.8	4,862.0
Money (M1)	588.4	589.0	717.4	745.4	790.6	910.3	880.3	961.4	1,088.5
Currency with the public	245.2	253.9	272.7	270.1	283.0	309.0	295.8	312.8	344.5
Private sector demand deposits	343.2	335.2	444.6	475.2	507.7	601.3	584.5	648.6	744.0

Table 3 *(concluded)*

	December 31								
	1990	1991	1992	1993	1994	1995	1996	1997	1998
Quasi money	1,861.1	2,073.8	2,150.8	2,400.1	2,602.1	2,961.5	3,065.5	3,361.4	3,773.5
Private sector savings deposits	1,017.7	1,119.1	1,184.5	1,397.6	1,571.1	1,737.0	1,828.9	1,937.8	2,127.6
Private sector time deposits	690.5	768.5	759.6	766.4	768.1	899.8	890.6	993.9	1,168.6
Private sector foreign currency deposits	152.9	186.3	206.7	236.0	262.9	324.7	346.1	429.7	477.4
Memorandum item:									
ECCB net foreign assets (in U.S. dollars)	196.4	208.5	266.2	261.8	253.8	303.1	281.0	302.1	353.0

Source: Eastern Caribbean Central Bank.
[1] Includes Anguilla and Montserrat.
[2] Includes social security systems.

Table 4. ECCB Area: Condensed Balance Sheet and Backing Ratio
(In millions of Eastern Caribbean dollars)

	December 31								
	1990	1991	1992	1993	1994	1995	1996	1997	1998
Total assets	743.5	790.2	911.9	883.7	879.4	1,006.0	954.4	990.5	1,142.20
External assets	543.8	590.1	746.6	719.5	698.1	836.3	778.7	823.7	957.5
Of which:									
On account of banker's fixed deposits	62.1	42.6	34.2	34.2	28.4	63.1	14.4	12.9	30.6
Domestic assets	199.7	200.1	165.2	164.3	181.3	169.6	175.8	166.8	184.7
Total liabilities	743.5	790.2	911.9	883.7	879.4	1,006.0	954.4	990.5	1,142.2
Demand liabilities	584.5	630.0	734.5	692.8	721.3	777.3	780.0	821.7	949.0
Bankers' fixed deposits	62.1	42.6	34.2	34.2	28.4	63.1	14.4	12.9	30.6
Net worth and other liabilities	96.9	117.7	143.2	156.8	129.7	165.6	160.0	156.0	162.6
Of which:									
General reserve	33.5	42.0	45.8	51.9	51.9	51.9	51.9	51.9	51.9
Other reserves	3.8	25.5	39.3	61.3	63.2	54.4	74.6	67.6	70.6
Memorandum items:									
Backing ratio (in percent)[1]	82.4	86.9	97.0	98.9	92.9	99.5	98.0	98.7	97.7
Calculated foreign assets reserve ratio[2]	82.1	86.4	96.9	98.9	92.7	99.5	97.9	98.7	97.7

Source: Eastern Caribbean Central Bank.
[1] Backing ratio defined as: (external assets - bankers' fixed deposits)/demand liabilities.
[2] The foreign assets reserve ratio is defined as: (ECCB external assets less bankers' fixed deposits less liabilities to international institutions and central banks) divided by (demand liabilities less liabilities to international institutions and central banks).

quirements (including marginal required reserves), which can vary by deposit type.

Credit ceilings have never been used in practice, and since its inception the ECCB has maintained a uniform reserve requirement of 6 percent on all deposits. Prior to March 1994, commercial banks were required to hold, for four consecutive weeks, 6 percent of average deposits for the four preceding weeks. However, this requirement was modified in March 1994 when the ECCB adopted weekly maintenance periods and began basing required reserves on average weekly deposits. Commercial bank reserves are unremunerated, as are excess reserves if held in EC dollar deposits. Shortly after its inception, however, in a situation of high world interest rates, the ECCB began encouraging commercial banks to invest foreign currency within the region by remunerating bankers' U.S. dollar deposits at internationally competitive interest rates.[11] The ECCB moreover permits

---
[11] There is a 24-hour/7-day call account facility, as well as 1, 2, 3, and 6-month deposit facilities. Already under ECCA, a pound sterling deposit facility for banks was established in 1968.

II THE FINANCIAL SYSTEM

Table 5. Selected ECCB and International Interest Rates
(Percent per annum)

	1991	1992	1993	1994	1995	1996	1997	1998
ECCB[1]								
Deposit rates for commercial banks								
Call	3.8	2.8	2.7	5.8	5.3	5.4	5.5	4.9
One-month	4.7	3.3	3.0	5.9	5.5	5.4	5.7	5.3
Three-month	4.2	3.3	3.1	6.2	5.4	5.4	5.5	4.9
Six-month	4.2	3.5	3.3	6.8	5.3	5.4	5.5	4.8
Lending rates								
Overdraft rate[2]	10.5	10.5	10.5	10.5	10.5	10.5	10.5	10.5
Discount rate	10.0	10.0	9.0	9.0	9.0	8.0	8.0	8.0
Advances to government	6.5	6.5	6.5	6.5	6.5	6.5	6.5	6.5
Interbank market (lending bank)	5.0	5.0	5.0	5.0	5.0	5.0	5.0	5.0
Interbank market (borrowing bank)	5.3	5.3	5.3	5.3	5.3	5.3	5.3	5.3
United States[1]								
Discount rate	3.5	3.0	3.0	4.8	5.3	5.0	5.0	4.5
LIBOR[3]								
Three-month	5.1	3.6	3.4	6.0	5.9	5.5	5.9	5.3
(Difference from ECCB three-month rate)	0.9	0.3	0.3	−0.3	0.4	0.1	0.4	0.4

Sources: Eastern Caribbean Central Bank, and IFS.
[1]Based on end-of-period rates.
[2]Overdraft rate on government operating accounts.
[3]Based on average Libor on U.S. dollars deposits over the fourth quarter.

bankers' deposits to be exchanged upon demand at the official cross-rate of EC$2.70 per U.S. dollar. This policy has helped to discourage bank capital outflows. During 1991–98, the three-month deposit rate was, on average, 0.3 percentage point lower than the LIBOR three-month rate (Table 5).

In 1986, the ECCB created an *interbank market* to enable commercial banks with excess reserves at the central bank to make loans for periods of up to 30 days to banks with reserve deficiencies, boosting overall liquidity management.[12] Borrowing banks are required to provide collateral (held by the central bank) in the form of fixed deposits, treasury bills, or other acceptable securities. Loans are brokered and guaranteed by the ECCB while the anonymity of both the borrowing and lending banks is preserved. This unique arrangement was designed, given the heterogeneous nature of the banking industry and the large disparity in bank size, to facilitate transactions regardless of bank ownership and size. Moreover, given the banking industry's limited technological capability, the central bank's involvement in the interbank market also helps to minimize banks' search and information costs, as the ECCB matches bids and offers across member territories. The rates in this interbank market have been fixed by the ECCB since the inception of the facility. Borrowing banks pay a rate of 5.25 percent, lending banks receive 5 percent, and the ECCB retains the margin of 25 basis points to cover the cost of intermediation.

In 1988, the ECCB established a *rediscount window for treasury bills*, essentially a secondary market for treasury bills, as an inducement to commercial banks to invest in government securities. Through this window, the Bank makes its portfolio of domestic treasury bills, obtained under the existing credit lines to member governments, available to commercial banks at rediscount rates unchanged since the inception of the facility[13] and discounts the bills at the banks' discretion. Operations with commercial banks through the rediscount window do not violate existing ECCB country credit limits as all such transactions are currently conducted through

---

[12]There is also a private interbank market, as described in Chapter IV.

[13]Commercial banks can rediscount treasury bills with the ECCB as follows: 1–29 days at a rate of 6.58 percent; 30–60 days at a rate of 6.65 percent; and 61–91 days at a rate of 6.71 percent. However, in practice the ECCB does not regularly rediscount bills maturing within 1–29 days.

the secondary market, and the volume is limited by the ECCB holdings of treasury bills.

The *discount rate* is intended to influence bank lending rates and thereby the level of economic activity by conveying the ECCB's policy stance through the announcement effect, but in practice it has been changed infrequently. It was last altered in August 1996, when it was lowered from 9 percent to 8 percent. Because the discount rate is above the rediscount rate for treasury bills, banks do not use the discount window.[14]

Most commercial bank interest rates are unregulated; the ECCB established, however, a 4 percent *minimum savings deposit rate* in 1984 with the aim of encouraging small savers. Since this policy was first instituted, there have been instances when the interest rate on short-term time deposits was below the 4 percent minimum savings rate, indicating that the statutory minimum was effectively binding. The result has been an increased demand for savings deposits (see Table 3).

Financial Institutions[15]

The onshore financial institutions as a whole held EC$8 billion in assets as of mid-1997. The bulk was held by commercial banks (72.5 percent of total assets in the region), with the remainder held by the social security funds (16 percent), credit unions (5 percent), development banks (3 percent), life insurance companies (2 percent), and general insurance companies (1.5 percent).

Historically, the financial systems of the Eastern Caribbean states have been dominated by *commercial banks*. The market comprises 44 banks; 23 branches of foreign-owned banks, 17 private local banks (including locally incorporated subsidiaries of foreign banks), two government-owned banks (one each in St. Lucia and St. Vincent and the Grenadines) and two government-controlled banks (one each in Dominica and St. Kitts and Nevis) (Table 6). The industry is heterogeneous in ownership as well as in scale of operations, with the smallest banks maintaining assets of under EC$50 million in 1997, while the largest have assets in excess of EC$300 million. With the rapid rise in their numbers since independence, locally incorporated banks now account for more than 50 percent of total bank assets.

The World Bank has identified two major constraints on the financial system of the ECCB region: *fragmentation* and *fractionalization*.[16] Intraterritory *fractionalization* stems from the proliferation of small-sized, inefficient financial institutions characterized by scale diseconomies that, in the case of commercial banks, contribute to high interest rate spreads (Table 7). Financial fragmentation also prevents the best allocation of resources, producing poorly diversified, small-scale institutions that are characterized both by high costs and a limited capacity to diversify risk.

The sources of *interterritory fragmentation* include the tendency of local financial institutions to constrain their investment to their host country— reinforced by tradition, and a number of established licensing, disclosure, and tax procedures; *legal restrictions*, including the Alien Landholding Acts, which restrict foreign (including intra-OECS) ownership of domestic assets such as real estate and majority equity ownership positions in local enterprises; *differential tax policies* for residents of each country and nonresidents, such as the application of withholding taxes on the payment of profits and interest to nonresidents and foreigners, and tax exemption of interest on government securities and on domestic bank deposits for residents only in most member states; and *prohibitions on residents' purchases of foreign currency securities or real estate abroad*, as well as other limits on outward capital flows.[17] Table 8 summarizes capital account restrictions pertaining to the ECCB member states (as of end-December 1997) and shows the great disparity in the nature and extent of the restrictions on both residents of other member states and residents from outside the region. Many of these restrictions are in the process of being revised as part of legislative reforms being undertaken to support the development of a single financial space (see Chapter III).

The *social security systems* account for the next largest share of financial assets in the region. Although the systems are not fully funded, they have acquired sizable surpluses, since participation is mandatory, and the plans and the populations are relatively young. Most of these resources are either held in commercial bank deposits—largely government securities mostly at government-owned banks but also other financial institutions—or in fixed income instruments. Thus, the funds are sometimes used to finance the government, either directly or indirectly.

---

[14]The discount rate and the other administered rates are reviewed at each meeting of the Monetary Council.

[15]This section draws on a report of the World Bank, *OECS Financial Sector Review*, May 1998 (gray cover).

[16]*OECS Financial Sector Review*, pp. 2–5.

[17]These restrictions apply in the case of Grenada, Dominica, St. Kitts and Nevis, St. Lucia, and St. Vincent and the Grenadines.

II THE FINANCIAL SYSTEM

Table 6. ECCB Area: List of Commercial Banks by Territory

	Bank (Year of Entry)		
	Foreign Branch	Private Local[1]	Government Owned
Anguilla	Barclays Bank (1968)	Caribbean Commercial Bank (1976) National Bank of Anguilla (1984) Scotiabank Anguilla (1991)	
Antigua and Barbuda	Bank of Nova Scotia (1961) Barclays Bank (1837) Caribbean Banking Corporation (1992) CIBC Caribbean Ltd. (1965) Royal Bank of Canada (1915)	Antigua & Barbuda Investment Bank (1990) Antigua Commercial Bank (1956) Bank of Antigua (1982) Swiss American National Bank (1981)	
Dominica	Bank of Nova Scotia (1988) Banque Francaise Commercial (1979) Barclays Bank (1837) Royal Bank of Canada (1915)		National Commercial Bank (1978) (51 percent government owned)
Grenada	Barclays Bank (1837)	Grenada Bank of Commerce (1983)[2] Bank of Nova Scotia (1963) Grenada Co-operative Bank (1933) National Commercial Bank (1979)[3]	
Montserrat	Barclays Bank (1964) Royal Bank of Canada (1917)	Bank of Montserrat (1988)	
St. Kitts and Nevis	Bank of Nova Scotia (1982) Barclays Bank (1837) Royal Bank of Canada (1915)	Bank of Nevis (1985) Caribbean Banking Corporation (1955)[4]	St. Kitts-Nevis-Anguilla National Bank (1971) (60 percent government owned)
St. Lucia	Bank of Nova Scotia (1964) Barclays Bank (1837) CIBC Caribbean Ltd. (1969) Royal Bank of Canada (1960)	Caribbean Banking Corporation (1993) St. Lucia Co-operative Bank (1938)	National Commercial Bank (1981)
St. Vincent and the Grenadines	Bank of Nova Scotia (1977) Barclays Bank (1837) CIBC Caribbean Ltd. (1964)	Caribbean Banking Corporation (1985)	National Commercial Bank (1977)

Source: Eastern Caribbean Central Bank.
[1]Includes locally incorporated subsidiaries of foreign banks.
[2]The government of Grenada began privatizing this bank in 1992. The government currently holds 10 percent of the shares.
[3]This bank was privatized in 1996.
[4]Formerly the Nevis Co-operative Bank.

Table 7. ECCB Area: Weighted Commercial Bank Interest Rates[1]
(Percent per annum)

	1991	1992	1993	1994	1995	1996	1997	1998
Antigua and Barbuda								
Weighted deposit rate	5.9	5.3	4.7	4.2	4.1	4.2	4.5	4.4
Weighted loan rate	12.6	12.8	13.3	13.3	12.5	12.3	12.1	12.3
Weighted reducing balance rate	12.6	12.8	12.4	12.6	11.8	11.7	11.7	11.7
Weighted add-on loan rate	0.0	0.0	15.6	15.9	14.6	14.4	14.5	14.1
Spread between loan and deposit rate	6.7	7.5	8.6	9.1	8.4	8.1	9.6	7.8
Dominica								
Weighted deposit rate	3.9	3.4	3.9	4.1	4.2	4.3	4.3	4.0
Weighted loan rate	11.6	11.6	12.1	11.8	11.5	11.5	11.0	11.2
Weighted reducing balance rate	11.1	11.2	11.7	11.0	10.8	11.0	10.5	10.5
Weighted add-on loan rate	16.8	16.8	16.8	16.2	16.1	16.5	16.6	17.2
Spread between loan and deposit rate	7.7	8.2	8.2	7.7	7.3	7.2	6.7	7.2
Grenada								
Weighted deposit rate	4.5	4.2	3.7	3.6	3.8	3.8	4.0	4.3
Weighted loan rate	12.2	12.7	11.5	10.0	10.4	10.1	11.5	11.8
Weighted reducing balance rate	12.2	12.7	11.3	9.5	10.0	9.7	11.4	11.7
Weighted add-on loan rate	0.0	0.0	14.2	14.3	14.0	13.7	13.1	13.2
Spread between loan and deposit rate	7.7	8.5	7.9	6.4	6.7	6.3	7.5	7.6
St. Kitts and Nevis								
Weighted deposit rate	5.4	6.0	4.0	4.0	4.0	4.0	4.1	4.2
Weighted loan rate	10.7	11.1	10.6	11.0	10.8	11.0	11.3	11.3
Weighted reducing balance rate	10.7	11.1	10.6	10.8	10.6	10.7	10.6	10.7
Weighted add-on loan rate	0.0	0.0	10.9	12.0	11.6	12.1	14.9	15.4
Spread between loan and deposit rate	5.3	5.1	6.6	7.0	6.8	7.0	7.2	7.1
St. Lucia								
Weighted deposit rate	4.5	4.3	3.9	4.0	4.2	4.6	4.6	4.8
Weighted loan rate	12.7	12.9	12.3	10.3	12.7	12.9	12.8	11.2
Weighted reducing balance rate	12.7	12.9	10.8	8.6	11.5	11.8	11.7	10.0
Weighted add-on loan rate	0.0	0.0	16.8	18.7	17.4	18.7	17.5	16.7
Spread between loan and deposit rate	8.3	8.6	8.3	6.3	8.5	8.4	8.1	6.5
St. Vincent and the Grenadines								
Weighted deposit rate	4.0	3.8	3.9	3.9	4.1	4.1	4.2	4.4
Weighted loan rate	11.2	11.3	12.0	11.7	11.1	11.2	11.4	11.4
Weighted reducing balance rate	11.2	11.3	11.6	11.1	10.5	10.6	10.8	11.3
Weighted add-on loan rate	0.0	0.0	14.8	14.9	14.5	14.5	14.4	14.5
Spread between loan and deposit rate	7.2	7.5	8.1	8.1	7.0	7.1	7.2	7.0

Source: Eastern Caribbean Central Bank.
[1] Annual averages shown are based on end-of-quarter rates.

Credit unions are the third largest group of financial institutions. There are 75 credit unions that—with the exception of one relatively large institution in Dominica with a market share of almost 25 percent—are micro-entities with less than EC$5 million in assets. About half their lending is for consumer loans, one third for mortgages, and the remainder is for loans to business and agriculture. Supervision of credit unions is not undertaken by a centralized body, but is carried out by the Registrars of Cooperatives of each state.

The region's state-owned *development banks* were established to provide medium- to long-term financing primarily for government-initiated projects that might be considered unattractive by the banking system. Since their primary source of funds is deposits of short- to medium-term maturity, commercial banks tend to specialize in short-term collateralized lending, which is not considered suitable for project financing. With more than half of commercial bank credit going to the trade and distribution sectors, as well as loans for personal use, development banks aim to assist the agricultural, manufacturing, and other production sectors to promote economic diversification.

Some development banks have been plagued by nonperforming loans—partly because of difficulties

II THE FINANCIAL SYSTEM

Table 8. ECCB Area: Selected Current and Capital Account Restrictions

	St. Kitts and Nevis	St. Lucia	St. Vincent and the Grenadines
Payments for invisible transactions and current transfers	Effective October 1, 1997, prior approval of the MOF is required for all transactions exceeding EC$250,000. All payments and transfers, except for the remittance of profits and dividends, are subject to quantitative and indicative limits and/or bona fide tests.	Effective November 15, 1997, prior approval is required for transactions exceeding EC$250,000, except for payments for travel, subscriptions, and membership fees.	Payments for invisibles related to authorized imports are not restricted. Effective January 1, 1998, other payments exceeding EC$250,000 must be approved by the MOF. Approval is granted routinely.
	Profits and dividends may be remitted in full, subject to confirmation of registration by the Commissioner of Inland Revenue for income tax purposes.	With the approval of the MFSN, profits may be remitted in full, subject to confirmation by the Comptroller of Inland Revenue that local tax liabilities have been discharged. However, in cases where profits are deemed to be high, the Ministry of Finance, Statistics, and Negotiating (MFSN) reserves the right to phase remittances over a reasonable period.	There are quantitative limits on payments for travel. The limits are the equivalent of EC$2,500 a year for travel outside the ECCB area and EC$6,000 a year for business travel. These allocations may be increased with the authorization of the MOF.
Controls on capital and money markets	Since October 1, 1997, individuals are permitted to purchase up to EC$250,000 without exchange control approval. All outward capital transfers exceeding that amount require exchange control approval.	Outward transfers exceeding EC$100,000 require Exchange control approval	All outward transfers require Exchange control approval.
a. On capital market securities	No restrictions on bonds or other debt securities. The following restrictions apply to shares or other securities of a participating nature:	No restrictions on bonds or other debt securities. The following restrictions apply to shares or other securities of a participating nature:	No restrictions on bonds or other debt securities. The following restrictions apply to shares or other securities of a participating nature:
Purchase locally by non-residents	For purchases of equity shares an Aliens Land Holding License is required	n.a.	n.a.
Sale or issue locally by non-residents	Foreign exchange approval is required from the MOF for amounts exceeding EC$250,000	n.a.	n.a.
Purchase abroad by residents	Same regulations as for sale or issue of capital market securities by nonresidents.	Yes.	Residents are not normally permitted to purchase foreign currency securities abroad for private purposes.
Sale or issue abroad by residents		n.a.	n.a.
b. On money market instruments Purchase locally by non-residents		n.a.	n.a.
Sale or issue locally by non-residents	Same regulations apply as for capital market securities.	n.a.	n.a.
Purchase abroad by residents	Same regulations apply as for capital market securities.	Yes.	Yes.
Sale or issue abroad by residents		n.a.	n.a.

Selected Restrictions

c. On collective investment securities		
Purchase locally by non-residents	Same regulations apply as for capital market securities.	n.a.
Sale or issue locally by non-residents	Same regulations apply as for capital market securities.	n.a.
Sale or issue abroad by residents	The seller of instruments has to be licensed under the Banking Act, and transfers abroad in excess of EC$250,000 require approval from the MOF.	n.a.
Purchase abroad by residents		Yes.
Controls on derivatives and other instruments.		
Purchase abroad by residents		n.a.
Purchase locally by non-residents		These transactions require approval from the MFSN. A person who has not resided in St. Lucia for three consecutive years is declared a nonresident.
Sale or issue locally by nonresidents		n.a.
Sale or issue abroad by residents		n.a.
Controls on credit operations		
a. Commercial credits		
By residents to nonresidents	These credits require approval of the MFSN. Applications for nonresident loans are submitted by the authorized dealer (or other financial intermediary) to the MFSN on behalf of the applicant.	MOF approval is required.
To residents from nonresidents	Yes.	n.a.
b. Financial credits		
By residents to nonresidents	MOF approval and payment of a 2.5 percent Alien's Loans Levy is required for these transactions.	MOF approval is required.
To residents from non-residents	Approval from the MOF is required for foreign exchange exceeding EC$250,000.	n.a.
c. Guarantees, sureties, and financial backup facilities	Approval from the MOF is required for foreign exchange exceeding EC$250,000.	n.a.
By residents to nonresidents	Yes.	
To residents from non-residents	Yes.	
Controls on direct investment		
a. Outward direct investment	Approval from the MOF is required for foreign exchange exceeding EC$250,000.	Yes.
b. Inward direct investment	Investments in equity require an Alien Landholding License.	Yes.

II THE FINANCIAL SYSTEM

Table 8 (concluded)

	St. Kitts and Nevis	St. Lucia	St. Vincent and the Grenadines
Controls on liquidation of direct investment	The remittance of proceeds from the liquidation of direct investments is permitted, subject to the discharge of any liabilities related to the investment. The transfer of proceeds exceeding EC$250,000 requires MOF approval.		The remittance of proceeds is permitted, subject to the discharge of any liabilities related to the investment.
Controls on real estate transactions			
a. Purchase abroad by residents	Purchasing real estate for private purposes is not normally permitted	Yes.	
b. Purchase locally by nonresidents	n.a.	Nonresidents who purchase property are taxed at a higher rate than residents. Amounts exceeding EC$250,000 require approval for repatriation of estate proceeds.	Yes.
c. Sale locally by nonresidents	n.a.		
Controls on personal capital movements			
Loans			
By residents to nonresidents			
To residents from nonresidents			
Gifts, endowments, inheritances, and legacies			
By residents to nonresidents			
Settlements of debts abroad by immigrants			
Transfer of assets			
Transfer abroad by emigrants			
Provisions specific to commercial banks and other credit institutions			
a. Borrowing abroad		Yes.	Any borrowing abroad to finance domestic operations requires approval of Ministry of Finance.
b. Maintenance of accounts abroad		Yes.	n.a.
c. Lending to nonresidents (financial or commercial credits)	MOF approval and payment of 2.5 percent Aliens Loan Levy.	There are controls on loans exceeding EC$250,000	n.a.

Selected Restrictions

d. Lending locally in foreign exchange	MOF approval is required, which is granted only in the case of projects generating foreign exchange to service the loan. The purchase of locally issued securities denominated in foreign currencies requires MOF approval.	n.a.
e. Purchase of locally issued securities denominated in foreign exchange	n.a.	n.a.
f. Investment regulations		n.a.
g. Open foreign exchange position limits		n.a.
h. Differential treatment of deposit accounts held by nonresidents.	n.a.	n.a.
i. Differential treatment of deposit accounts in foreign exchange.	n.a.	n.a.
j. Open foreign exchange position limits	n.a.	
Provisions specific to institutional investors	No regulations exist.	
Other restrictions imposed by securities laws	No.	

Source: *IMF Exchange Arrangements and Exchange Restrictions: 1998 Annual Report.*
Notes: "Yes" connotes that there is a restriction or control; "no" implies that the particular measure is not restricted or controlled; and "n.a." means that the information is not available.

encountered in making adequate feasibility assessments in the case of projects with long gestation periods of approximately three to five years. In response, the Caribbean Development Bank (CDB) has financed institutional strengthening programs to restructure the management and operational practices of several development banks, based on the principle that they should operate according to commercial standards with international best practices for governance and management, capitalization and financing, and regulation. Under such programs, investment decisions are made by a professional and independent board of directors, and bank managerial operations are overseen by external auditors.

Life insurance and general insurance companies account for the remaining share of the region's financial assets. Providers of general insurance tend to specialize in property insurance, linked to catastrophe coverage (including fire and natural disasters) under comprehensive home and commercial policies, as well as in auto insurance. Local companies reinsure up to 85 percent of the risk they underwrite with foreign companies and earn commission based on reinsurance premiums. The current regulation and supervision of this industry needs to be strengthened, with focus on the adequacy of capitalization to cover the 15 percent of risk retained by local insurers and on the reliability of the foreign companies responsible for the other 85 percent.[18] This is of particular concern given the recent substantial increase in new entrants into the industry (because of rising profitability associated with an increase in reinsurance premiums), that in turn has resulted in greater industry fractionalization.

The life insurance industry, dominated by two major companies, has grown over the past decade because of the expansion in mortgage lending (as mortgage holders are typically required to purchase life insurance). Industry participants have argued that a broader availability of investment securities would facilitate insurance rate reductions by enhancing the yield of their portfolios, and stimulate the demand for various insurance products. The industry, therefore, seems well-poised to benefit from the new investment opportunities created by the ECCB's money and capital markets development initiatives.

Regulatory Framework

Legal Requirements

The ECCB's regulatory and supervisory jurisdiction over commercial banks and other licensed financial institutions (including finance companies and offshore banks affiliated with local banks) is established in the 1983 ECCB Agreement Act (Articles 4 and 35), as well as in the Uniform Banking Act (UBA) approved by member governments in 1991. The Banking Act was amended in 1993, broadening its scope to include all licensed nonbank financial institutions other than credit unions and insurance companies. In 1993, an amendment to the 1983 ECCB Agreement gave the central bank emergency powers to intervene in failing financial institutions that are of systemic importance.[19] In such situations, the ECCB now has power to investigate and to take whatever steps necessary to protect depositors, including the confiscation and sale of assets. The ECCB does not have direct supervisory jurisdiction over nonbank financial institutions not licensed under the Banking Act, such as credit unions, offshore banks with no local onshore affiliation, insurance companies, development banks, and other financial institutions that are regulated by different acts and authorities in the national territories.

In an attempt to harmonize the regulatory framework faced by credit unions and other cooperatives, member countries are in the process of ratifying the "Harmonized Cooperatives Societies Bill." Approval has been obtained in the case of Antigua and Barbuda, Dominica, Grenada, St. Kitts and Nevis, and St. Vincent and The Grenadines, but is still pending in the other three territories. In addition, there is ongoing research, being conducted by an insurance advisor, to develop an appropriate regulatory framework for the insurance industry.

Legal requirements faced by all licensed financial institutions include a minimum paid-up capital requirement, the maintenance of a statutory reserve fund, restrictions on lending to related parties, a restriction on large credit exposure, restrictions governing the nature of bank investments, and satisfaction of a reserve requirement.

- The minimum *paid-up capital* requirement for newly established locally incorporated banks is EC$5 million. The applicable minimum paid-up capital requirement for nonbank financial institutions is determined by the relevant ministry of finance in consultation with the ECCB, but it should not be less than EC$1 million. Foreign branch banks (namely, existing branches of foreign banks) are subject to an *assigned minimum capital requirement* of 5 percent of the branch's

---

[18]*OECS Financial Sector Review*.

[19]A necessary condition for the ECCB to intervene is that the failure of a financial institution has the potential to put "the financial system of any of the territories of the participating Governments in danger of disruption, substantial damage, injury or impairment" (Article 5B. (2)). This amendment was introduced in order to enable to ECCB to respond appropriately to the failure of the Bank of Montserrat in 1993 (see Chapter V).

deposit liabilities, applied annually. This requirement is satisfied by the provision of a "letter of comfort" from the parent institution certifying that the assigned capital is being held in the books of the head office on behalf of each branch bank.

- Financial institutions are required to maintain a *Statutory Reserve Fund* equivalent to 100 percent of paid-up capital, and to transfer a minimum of 20 percent of annual profits to the Statutory Reserve Fund account until the fund is equal to the paid-up capital.

- Financial institutions are prohibited from providing unsecured credit to directors, external auditors/examiners and persons holding 10 percent or more of shares in the institution, except if a waiver is granted by the minister of finance after consultation with the ECCB. Credit facilities granted to such individuals cannot be provided at rates more favorable than those offered to other customers. Financial institutions are also prohibited from lending against their own shares.

- The stock of unsecured loans to any individual or group of related individuals must not exceed 15 percent of a bank's unimpaired capital and reserves, but this restriction can be waived if loans are secured by acceptable collateral valued at 20 percent or more of the loan amount, and/or upon a decision by a country's minister of finance after consultation with the central bank.

- The Banking Act contains provisions that limit the nature of banks' commercial activity, including constraints on buying real estate, except for purposes of business expansion, and ownership interests in business ventures.

- Licensed commercial banks must comply with the 6 percent *reserve requirement*, on both Eastern Caribbean dollar and foreign currency deposits.

Prudential Guidelines

The ECCB first introduced *prudential guidelines* conforming to international best practices (as defined in the Basel Committee's banking supervision guidelines) in November 1994. These guidelines are, in many cases, more stringent than the requirements of the UBA. The prudential guidelines have been adapted over time[20] and at present they govern large credit exposures, provisioning requirements for nonperforming loans, an aggregate limit of 10 percent on the ratio of nonperforming assets to total assets

(this limit has been in effect since 1987), the suspension of interest on nonperforming assets, and compliance with capital adequacy standards adapted by the CARICOM Bank Supervisors from the Basel Committee guidelines.

- Prudential guidelines on *large credit exposures*, issued in 1994, are consistent with the Basel Committee's 1991 recommendations and require financial institutions to limit their exposure to any single individual or group of related persons to 25 percent of paid-up capital and reserves irrespective of the security provided.[21, 22] Institutions found to be in violation of this are required to take immediate action to either reduce the exposure or increase the level of "Tier I capital" (see below).

- Under the *"harmonized approach" to loan provisioning* introduced in 1995, at least 70 percent of each financial institution's credit portfolio is subject to an annual review, at which time the quality of each loan is assessed and a grade is assigned that has associated with it a minimum provision level. This assessment is based on such criteria as the regularity and promptness and timeliness of debt-service payments; the presence and quality of collateral and/or other securitization; the degree of sensitivity to economic conditions; and the quality of the supporting loan documentation. Loans are then assigned the following labels, with the corresponding provisions: "pass," requiring no provision; "special mention," requiring no provision; "substandard" but fully secured by cash or government securities, which requires no provision; "substandard" with no securitization, requiring a 10 percent provision; "doubtful," requiring a 50 percent provision; and "loss," requiring a 100 percent provision. In addition, *a maximum tolerable limit of 10 percent on the ratio of nonperforming or "unsatisfactory" assets to total assets* was established. Loans are

---

[20]In particular, in July 1995 the ECCB introduced additional prudential guidelines (including stricter provisioning standards) and expanded the reporting requirements of banks.

[21]This guideline is more stringent than the corresponding stipulation in the UBA, since unlike the UBA the guidelines do not allow for exceptions from the stipulated 25 percent. Since the provisions of the UBA have legal precedence over the prudential guidelines, there is a recognized need to harmonize the two documents.

[22]In this respect, a "group of related persons" is defined as "two or more persons, . . . holding exposures from the same credit institution and of its subsidiaries, whether on a joint or separate basis, but who are mutually associated in that: (i) one of them holds directly or indirectly power of control over the other. . .or; (ii) their cumulated exposures represent to the credit institution a single risk in so much as they are interconnected with the likelihood that if one of them experiences financial problems the other or all of them are likely to encounter repayment difficulties. . . ." Relevant "interconnections" among persons include: "common ownership, common directors, cross guarantees, and direct commercial interdependency which cannot be substituted in the short term."

classified as nonperforming when they have been in arrears for 90 days or more.

- Under guidelines for *the suspension of interest on nonperforming assets*, banks are required to stop accruing interest on accounts that are 90 days or more in arrears, unless there is adequate security and full collection is expected within three months. Except in the case of loans to government or loans with a government-guarantee, banks are prohibited from accruing interest on overdrafts when the approved limit has been reached or when credits to the account are insufficient to cover interest accruals for at least a three-month period. In the case of government and government-guaranteed loans, accrual of interest is permitted up to the limit of the guarantee or up to the value of the collateral. A loan's accrual status is restored when all the arrears of principal and interest have been paid, and, in the case of overdrafts, accrual status is restored when the account is operating within the approved limit and all interest arrears have been cleared. Accrued, uncollected interest should be reflected in an "interest in suspense" account on the balance sheet.

- There are also guidelines governing the conditions under which loans and advances can be renegotiated because of weaknesses in the borrower's financial position or the emergence of payment arrears. These guidelines include considerations about the borrower's ability to service the loan under the new conditions and the adequacy of supporting securitization.

- Locally incorporated commercial banks are required to maintain the ratio of Tier I (or "core") capital to risk-weighted assets at a minimum of 8 percent.[23] This *capital adequacy* ratio was adapted by the CARICOM Bank Supervisors from the Basel Committee guidelines, with the aim to be somewhat more stringent than the Basel Committee. The latter was drafted with larger and better diversified banks in mind, and requires a ratio of *total* qualifying capital (Tier I and Tier II[24] capital less investments in financial subsidiaries not included in the group consolidation) to risk-weighted assets of 8 percent.

- The ECCB guidelines also specify a *liquidity requirement*, namely that the ratio of Tier I capital to deposits be not less than 1:20.

ECCB requirements are either in line with or exceed international best practices (although there are no requirements for foreign exchange exposure). Box 4 shows ECCB commercial bank prudential requirements and compares these requirements with the Basel Committee recommendations and with the 1996 recommendations made by the IMF's Monetary and Exchange Affairs Department in the context of its technical assistance.[25]

Monitoring

Monitoring compliance with these requirements is undertaken by the ECCB's Bank Supervision Department, which is organized into three units: on-site examination, off-site surveillance, and supervisory actions. The latter also monitors the activities of all financial institutions, including those not licensed under the Banking Act. The Banking Supervision Department provides technical assistance in capacity building to the national entities supervising credit unions and insurance companies. It also works closely with the various supervisory authorities of the member territories on the regulation of offshore banks without local onshore affiliation, and provides guidance as needed.[26]

On-site inspections of the locally incorporated banks are conducted every 18 months under normal circumstances, although the frequency is increased in the case of weak institutions. Loan portfolios are evaluated by ECCB bank examiners for the amount and terms of the loans, evaluation of the projects

---

[23]Tier I capital is comprised of paid-up ordinary share capital and surplus, paid-up perpetual noncumulative preference shares and share surplus; statutory reserves; capital reserves (excluding asset revaluations); general reserves (excluding reserves losses on assets); audited retained earnings (accumulated losses) *less* current year losses; bonus shares from capitalization of unrealized asset revaluation reserves; goodwill and other intangibles.

Risk weights for balance sheet items are as follows: (a) zero for foreign and domestic currency cash and government securities; (b) 20 percent for claims on domestic and foreign financial institutions; (c) 50 percent for fully secured real estate residential mortgages; and (d) 100 percent for other claims on the private sector and for real estate and equity investments. For off-balance sheet items: (a) zero risk is attached to claims (with or without government guarantees) on domestic and foreign government entities; (b) 20 percent to claims on domestic and approved foreign financial institutions, public sector entities and multilateral development banks; and (c) 100 percent to claims on the private sector and other institutions.

[24]Tier II capital consists of fixed asset revaluation reserves (limited to 20 percent of Tier I capital); general provisions/reserves for losses on assets (limited to 1.25 percent of total risk-weighted assets); paid-up perpetual cumulative preference shares and share surplus; bonus shares from capitalization of unrealized asset revaluation reserves; unaudited undivided profits; asset revaluation reserves; mandatory convertible debt instruments; other hybrid capital instruments; and subordinated term debt and limited life preference shares (limited to 50 percent of Tier I capital).

[25]*Bank Soundness and Macroeconomic Policy*, by C. J. Lindgren, G. Garcia, and M. I. Saal, IMF (1996), p.187.

[26]Dominica's legislature recently approved legislation that enables the ECCB to supervise its offshore banks (in accordance with the provisions of Article 41 of the ECCB Agreement Act).

Box 4. Prudential Requirements for Commercial Banks

Requirement	Basel Committee	IMF General Recommendations[1]	ECCB
Minimum capital for new banks	No guidance	US$1 million	EC$5 million (US$1.92 million)
Minimum capital adequacy ratio	Total capital to risk weighted assets of at least 8 percent	At least 8 percent; more in a high-risk environment	Tier I capital to risk weighted assets of at least 8 percent
Loans to one borrower	Could be best practice, but not more than 25 percent of total capital	At most 25 percent of total capital applied to single borrower or group of related borrowers	At most 25 percent of unimpaired capital and reserves irrespective of type of securitization
Lending to related parties	No guidance, but special attention needed	From 25 percent to 50 percent of total capital applied to related parties and in total no more than 100 percent	No more than 25 percent of unimpaired capital and reserves irrespective of type of securitization
Liquidity ratios	Guidelines on measuring and managing liquidity risk	Guidelines are necessary and ratios are useful	Tier I capital to deposits ratio of 1:20; cash reserves of 6 percent; unsatisfactory assets to total assets of 10 percent
Foreign exchange exposure	Position limits recommended	Limits necessary either as a ratio or in absolute terms	Cash reserve requirement of 6 percent of foreign currency deposits

[1]See *Bank Soundness and Macroeconomic Policy*, by C. J. Lindgren, G. Garcia, and M. I. Saal, IMF (1996), p. 187.

being financed, the quality of collateral, and the timeliness of debt-service payments by borrowers. If a commercial bank is found to be in violation of ECCB prudential guidelines, a "memorandum of understanding" or "letter of commitment" is signed between the bank and the ECCB stipulating a schedule of corrective actions to be taken within a specified time. The ECCB then does a follow-up inspection upon implementation of the required corrective actions. However, as discussed below, the ECCB lacks the legislative authority to issue cease and desist orders outside of the emergency powers stipulated in the ECCB's Amendment Order No. 48 of 1993. This is particularly relevant since the emergency legislation is applicable only in the event of a systemic banking crisis.

Off-site reporting requirements for commercial banks include the provision of balance sheets (monthly); a report on loans and advances by sector (quarterly); the provision of detailed information on bank investment portfolios, including type, currency, country of issue, interest rate, and maturity date (quarterly); income statements (quarterly); annual reports; large exposure and liquidity schedules (quarterly); and information on past-due and nonperforming loans and other problem credits (quarterly). There are separate reporting requirements for investments administered by banks as fund managers.

III Money and Capital Market Development Initiatives

The goal of the *money and capital markets development initiatives* being sponsored by the ECCB is to create a "single financial space" within the Eastern Caribbean region. This is seen as the fulfillment of the objective set in Article 4, Section 3 of the ECCB Agreement requiring the Bank to "promote credit and exchange conditions and a sound financial structure conducive to . . . balanced growth and development." The program seeks to achieve greater economies of scale in the region's financial operations by integrating the regions' financial markets. It also aims to broaden and deepen the financial markets and to enhance the effectiveness and efficiency of the mobilization of domestic and foreign savings to foster economic growth.

The ECCB perceives its role to be that of a catalyst to establish the needed financial institutions and markets and, at the outset, the Bank plans to assume an active role as market maker and a key player in the operation of these markets. The ECCB is determined to safeguard the fiscal and monetary discipline imposed by its quasi-currency board arrangement, and plans to divest equity participation in the new and proposed financial institutions (discussed below) once successfully launched.

Each element of the money and capital markets development program is designed to fill a particular niche in the financial sector:

- The *money market program* has two components. The first is the development of a fully integrated market for government short-term paper (the treasury bills market), in the form of a fully *integrated* primary and secondary *Regional Government Securities Market* (RGSM). Technical assistance for the RGSM was provided by the IMF in 1996 and 1997, and the ECCB is working with the member governments on getting operations started. The second is the establishment of a private money market (in negotiable certificates of deposit and other short-term private instruments). There has been little progress on this front, and not much is expected before the establishment of the call exchange (see below).

- The *capital market program* includes the *Eastern Caribbean Home Mortgage Bank* which provides a secondary market for residential mortgages; the establishment, within the next two years, of the *Eastern Caribbean Enterprise Fund*; the creation of an *Eastern Caribbean Securities Exchange* intended to provide a regional secondary market for shares (equities) and promote secondary trading of these securities; establishment of the *Eastern Caribbean Securities Regulatory Commission*, along with the supporting legal and regulatory framework that will provide for the regulation of the securities market; and the creation of an *Eastern Caribbean Unit Trust Company (ECUTC)*, a regional mutual fund investment company designed to facilitate the participation of small investors.

The RGSM program is being designed to develop, expand, and integrate the existing markets for the region's government securities (currently largely comprised of the issuance of three-month treasury bills by five of the eight ECCB member governments), thereby broadening the range of portfolio investment alternatives available to investors within the region. The program seeks to redress market segmentation that has limited the demand for government securities. The successful establishment of the government securities market is the vehicle chosen to bring about greater flexibility of interest rates in the region, driven by market determination of the yield on government securities (see Chapter V). It is expected that this will provide governments with enlarged access to domestic sources of financing as a more cost-effective alternative to borrowing from commercial banks, particularly in the longer end of the market. Furthermore, long-term government bonds would broaden the range of investment alternatives for long-term savings generated by the region's pension funds and insurance companies.

While planning for the implementation of the RGSM, the ECCB has aimed to lay the groundwork for an integrated market by increasing its role

Money and Capital Market Development Initiatives

in managing government bond issues, administering member government sinking funds, providing advice on the terms and conditions of bond issues, facilitating payment of interest coupons via local commercial banks, announcing bond issues, and disseminating prospectuses and the relevant application forms. The Bank has also launched a publicity campaign to help promote acceptance of the RGSM program among potential investors. In addition, a *Regional Debt Coordinating Committee* comprising the Directors of Finance/Financial Secretaries of the member territories, has been appointed to regulate and help develop the RGSM.

While certain decisions have already been taken, for example, that the auctions will be uniform price auctions and that participation will be restricted initially to residents of the OECS states only, there are several organizational issues and supporting measures still to be addressed. Some of them are the need for uniform tax treatment of residents and non-residents of the ECCB area, agreement on arrangements for ensuring the availability of funds during the transition period in the event that some issues are undersubscribed, and various computerization and software-related issues.

Since its inception in 1995, the *Eastern Caribbean Home Mortgage Bank* (ECHMB) has helped mobilize liquidity for private sector investment by providing primary lenders (such as commercial banks, credit unions, building and loan associations, and development banks) with access to liquidity in exchange for the sale of their primary mortgages. The ECHMB, in addition, has expanded its scope of operations by making arrangements with some primary lenders who offer mortgages on its behalf. At end-January 2000, ECHMB's portfolio of mortgages amounted to EC$ 22.8 million.

The ECHMB has had six successful bond issues, including a bond for mortgages swap. Most of the bonds were subscribed by institutional investors and individuals in the member territories, as well as investors from Barbados. Bond issues outstanding as of end-1999 amounted to EC$56.1 million. ECHMB bonds provide investors with an investment alternative to commercial bank deposits. The institution has shown a steady growth in profitability. Its borrowing costs have been relatively low—the interest rate paid on the outstanding bonds issued ranges from 6.75–7.75 percent, while the benchmark lending rate is approximately 10.25 percent. The latter is still below most rates on the primary market, as the ECHMB has been able to pass on the savings from its low cost of funds and low overhead costs (owing to the wholesale nature of its operations) to its customers in the form of lower mortgage rates. Member governments of the ECCB area have awarded ECHMB bonds tax exempt status, thereby increasing the advantages of these instruments.

The *Eastern Caribbean Enterprise Fund (ECEF)*, still in the planning stage, is intended as a subregional investment/venture capital fund, that would raise domestic capital for private sector development as well as help organize and channel foreign investment capital from two existing regional investment funds—the Commonwealth Equity Fund (CEF) and the Caribbean Investment Fund (CIF)—and other international sources to viable private sector initiatives. The ECEF would provide venture capital in the form of debt and equity financing (both indirectly, through equity participation in financial institutions and other funds, and through direct equity participation in business firms) to private enterprises with primarily an export- or import-substituting focus. In so doing, it would try to manage risk by maintaining a portfolio balanced in relation to geographical origin and industrial orientation, new versus established enterprises, maturity structure of assets and liabilities, foreign exchange exposure (through judicious use of forward exchange rate cover), and debt versus equity investments.

The ECEF is not expected to start for some time. For the time being, the ECCB has decided to maintain, and focus on, the *Export Credit Guarantee Scheme (ECGS)*, which has been in operation since 1984 (but with interruptions). The ECGS provides partial (up to 80 percent) guarantees at a 1 percent charge for short-term (up to 180 days) commercial bank credits intended to provide pre- and post-shipment working capital for export firms. Some consideration is now being given to expanding the scheme's coverage to include a domestic production credit facility. The latter is being supported under the Multilateral Investment Facility of the Inter-American Development Bank (IDB). The ECCB has allocated EC$1 million toward the capitalization of such a fund, and the credit guarantees can be issued up to 20 times the capital base. The present contingent liability of the Export Credit Guarantee Scheme is EC$5 million. The ECGS was restructured within the last year, and now falls under the jurisdiction of the ECCB's Financial and Enterprise Development Unit (FEDU), which is charged with monitoring its performance. As part of these reforms, commercial banks are now bound by a credit ceiling of EC$100,000 and are required to consult with FEDU before using the scheme, as well as report to FEDU by the day after the transaction and submit monthly reports thereafter.

The *Eastern Caribbean Securities Exchange* (ECSE) is envisaged as the first regional electronic stock exchange in the Western Hemisphere. Funding for the ECSE project has been obtained from the IDB (via the CDB), and the project is scheduled to

III MONEY AND CAPITAL MARKET DEVELOPMENT INITIATIVES

be completed in 2000. Implementation will, however, require the elimination of a number of legal impediments, including the passage of uniform securities legislation in the member territories. Two subsidiary institutions of the ECSE will be created to provide electronic clearance, settlement, registration and custody of securities listed on the ECSE. They are the *Eastern Caribbean Central Securities Depository (ECCSD)* to provide clearance and settlement, as well as custody services, for intermediaries and custodian banks; and the *Eastern Caribbean Central Securities Registry (ECCSR)* to maintain the registers of securities holders on behalf of issuers and to provide a range of registry services.

These prospective money and capital markets initiatives would require the passage, by governments of member states, of important enabling legislative and regulatory reforms to cover tax harmonization; the Aliens Landholding Laws; Uniform Securities, Insurance, and Development Banks Laws; uniform accounting, reporting, and disclosure standards; and the harmonization and eventual elimination of various capital account restrictions.

The efficiency of the RGSM is likely to be constrained by the extensive differences in taxation policy across countries (both in terms of types and rates of taxation as well as the nature of exemptions granted), which is likely to impinge on the relative attractiveness of member countries' securities. The ECCB's Legal Unit has therefore recommended the harmonization of taxes on dividends and interest, and on profits and capital gains (as well as stamp duties). The St. Lucia model is upheld as an example to consider since it exempts nationals of member states from withholding requirements on tax on dividends, interest or discounts, leases, premiums, licenses, annuities, or other periodic payments. Although tax reform is not a prerequisite for starting the RGSM, until taxation policy is harmonized, differential tax treatment will have an important bearing on the operations of the market.

Alien landholding regulations restrict the holding of land by unlicensed aliens[27] and the holding of an interest in companies under alien control that are incorporated in any member state of the OECS in order to promote the establishment of locally owned companies. The legislation also imposes restrictions on trusts in favor of aliens. The administrative requirements for the issue, transfer, and maintenance of a license are cumbersome and may delay the processing of applications by investors. This has direct implications for the viability of the proposed Securities Exchange and the RGSM. A proposed draft Aliens Landholding Regulation Act would modify the existing Acts by changing the definition of the word "alien" so that only noncitizens of OECS member states would be considered alien. However, so far, the draft bill has not been approved by the legislatures. As an alternative, the ECCB has asked the member countries to consider exempting citizens of OECS member states from the provisions of the Act on a reciprocal basis.

A *Harmonized Companies Act* has been enacted by all member countries except St. Kitts and Nevis, where a similar act was already in force, and contains modern provisions governing the formation, registration, operations, and closure of companies. The Harmonized Companies Regulations, intended to facilitate the administration of the Companies Act, also have been approved by all member countries (except St. Kitts and Nevis). The regulations provide for standard forms to be presented to the Registrar of Companies; set out the fees for services provided in accordance with the Act, such as registration, the issuance of certificates, and searches; and require the filing of annual returns. The regulations also standardize the content of prospectuses, reports, financial statements, and the general by-laws of a company incorporated or continued under the Act.

---

[27]"Alien" is defined as any person who is not a citizen of that territory and companies owned by noncitizens.

IV Recent Economic Developments

Output, Employment, and Prices

The growth of real GDP in the OECS region declined from 3 percent in 1997 to a little more than 2 percent in 1998, with real GDP per capita growing at just over 1 percent (Table 9). The utilities and construction sectors registered strong gains (Table 10), supported by substantial public sector investment and private residential construction in most countries in the region. Tourism activity in 1995–96 suffered from the damage caused by hurricanes in the fall of 1995, but the number of stayover visitors and cruise ship passengers increased markedly in 1997–98, aided by improvements in port facilities, visits by larger cruise ships, and greater marketing efforts.

As tourism and other services have gained importance, the structure of the economy has continued to shift away from agriculture and manufacturing. The contribution of agriculture to GDP declined from 10½ percent in 1990–95 to about 8⅓ percent in 1996–98, while that of manufacturing remained at around 6 percent of GDP (Table 11). Agricultural production has been affected by high unit costs and bad weather, with banana output also hampered by quality problems and, mainly in Grenada, pests. More stringent quality requirements for export and the uncertain prospects for continued preferential access to the EU market have recently accelerated the exit of farmers from the banana industry (see below). Performance in other key crops (sugarcane, nutmeg, and cocoa) has been mixed. High production costs have also hindered the manufacturing sector, with increased competition from lower cost countries in export markets and the persistent decline in the demand for inputs from banana exporters recently affecting output adversely.

Official estimates indicate that the unemployment rate has been declining in most countries in recent years, but it remains high in some. Analyzing the severity of this problem is hampered by the lack of statistics on unemployment and wages. The information on wages that is readily available points to wage increases to government employees that outpaced inflation in most countries during 1996–98.

A slight deterioration in public sector saving accompanied by an expansion in public sector investment contributed to the widening of the external current account deficit during 1996–98. While gross national saving is estimated to have eroded markedly during this period, gross domestic investment has remained broadly unchanged at 31–32 percent of GDP (Table 12). Reported high investment rates in most countries may reflect inefficiencies, in part associated with large capital outlays in relation to the scale of operations required in small island economies, as well as statistical inaccuracies.

Inflation was relatively low during 1996–98, with the 12-month rate of increase in the consumer price index estimated at about 2⅔ percent in 1998 (Table 13), and about 2 percent in 1999. The moderate inflation reflects the slow rate of increase in import prices in recent years and the stability of the Eastern Caribbean dollar. Sporadic deviations from price stability have been temporary and largely associated with policy changes. Such was the case of St. Kitts and Nevis in 1997, when the rate of inflation rose temporarily following changes in tax policy. More recently, concerns have arisen that large public investment programs in certain countries and large increases in compensation for government employees in others, may be contributing to a less favorable price performance than that warranted by external conditions.

Banana Sector

The Windward Islands (Dominica, Grenada, St. Lucia, and St. Vincent and the Grenadines) have been exporting bananas to the United Kingdom since the early 1950s, and by the early 1960s bananas had become the most important economic activity. Banana production and exports from the Windward Islands, however, declined sharply after 1990. Output fell by half, from about 280,000 tons in 1990 to under 145,000 tons in 1998.[28] The decline was most severe in Grenada (Table 14).

---

[28]None of the Windward Islands has fulfilled its quota under the EU banana regime in any given year.

IV RECENT ECONOMIC DEVELOPMENTS

Table 9. ECCB Area: Output and Population Growth
(Annual percentage changes)

	1990	1991	1992	1993	1994	1995	1996	1997	1998
	\multicolumn{9}{c}{*Real GDP[1]*}								
ECCB area	4.7	0.7	3.9	2.6	3.0	0.7	2.7	3.1	2.3
Anguilla	7.0	−3.6	7.1	7.5	7.1	−4.1	3.5	9.2	5.5
Antigua and Barbuda	2.3	2.7	0.8	5.1	6.2	−5.0	6.1	5.6	3.9
Dominica	6.3	2.1	2.7	1.9	2.1	1.6	3.1	2.0	3.5
Grenada	5.2	3.6	1.1	−1.2	3.3	3.1	2.9	4.2	5.8
Montserrat	14.3	−20.9	2.7	2.5	0.9	−7.6	−21.4	−26.5	−3.2
St. Kitts and Nevis	3.1	2.3	3.1	5.4	5.4	3.5	5.9	7.3	1.6
St. Lucia	4.2	0.1	7.4	1.1	1.8	1.7	1.4	0.6	2.9
St. Vincent and the Grenadines	6.7	1.4	6.9	1.8	−2.9	8.3	1.2	3.1	5.7
	\multicolumn{9}{c}{*Population*}								
ECCB area	0.6	0.3	1.3	1.4	1.0	1.2	0.2	0.2	1.0
Anguilla	3.7	3.6	3.1	3.3	3.4	3.8	3.5	11.7	4.5
Antigua and Barbuda	0.0	0.1	1.3	1.4	1.2	1.8	1.5	0.1	0.9
Dominica	−0.4	−0.4	0.6	1.8	1.5	0.5	−0.1	1.9	0.5
Grenada	0.6	1.0	0.9	0.5	0.8	0.7	0.4	0.6	0.7
Montserrat	−0.4	−8.2	0.0	−3.8	−0.9	2.0	−25.8	−55.5	−5.8
St. Kitts and Nevis	−0.2	−2.1	4.1	2.0	−1.1	1.1	−2.9	0.0	0.1
St. Lucia	1.4	1.4	1.6	1.3	1.9	1.8	1.7	1.3	1.6
St. Vincent and the Grenadines	0.9	0.6	0.8	1.9	0.5	0.6	0.6	0.4	0.8
	\multicolumn{9}{c}{*Real Per Capita GDP*}								
ECCB area	4.1	0.4	2.6	1.2	2.0	−0.5	2.5	2.9	1.3
Anguilla	3.4	−7.3	4.0	4.1	3.7	−7.9	0.0	−2.5	1.0
Antigua and Barbuda	2.3	2.6	−0.4	3.7	4.9	−6.7	4.6	5.4	3.0
Dominica	6.7	2.5	2.2	0.0	0.6	1.1	3.2	0.1	2.9
Grenada	4.6	2.7	0.2	−1.7	2.5	2.4	2.5	3.6	5.1
Montserrat	14.7	−12.7	2.7	6.3	1.8	−9.6	4.4	29.0	2.5
St. Kitts and Nevis	3.3	4.3	−1.0	3.4	6.5	2.3	8.8	7.3	1.5
St. Lucia	2.8	−1.3	5.8	−0.3	−0.1	−0.1	−0.3	−0.7	1.3
St. Vincent and the Grenadines	5.7	0.8	6.1	−0.1	−3.4	7.7	0.6	2.7	4.9

Sources: Eastern Caribbean Central Bank, and IMF staff estimates.
[1]Data refer to growth of GDP at factor cost.

The decline in production and exports was caused by several factors. Low productivity and fruit quality have been persistent problems. More recently, there has been the uncertainty arising from the prospects of a less favorable EU banana import regime following the emergence of a single European market in 1993 and the legal challenges brought against this regime by Latin American producers and the United States in 1995 (Box 5). As a result, farmers have left the industry and planted acreage has declined. The price of bananas in the United Kingdom (the green market price) also fluctuated sharply during the 1990s, while the British pound depreciated against the U.S. dollar and hence, the EC dollar (see Table 14). In addition, output was affected by periodic natural disasters (droughts, tropical storms, and hurricanes) and strikes by growers (St. Lucia) or by port workers (St. Vincent and the Grenadines).

To address product quality problems, the Windward Islands Banana Growers Associations and WIBDECO[29] implemented a certified farmer program in 1996–97, with the technical and financial help of the EU. The objective is to certify a pool of farmers as capable of producing, processing, and packaging bananas to meet the requirements of the United Kingdom supermarket trade. By the end of

---

[29]WIBDECO, the Windward Islands Banana Development and Export Company, is a holding company jointly owned by the four governments of the Windward Islands and the four Banana Growers Associations (BGAs) on a 50–50 equity participation basis. WIBDECO loads the green bananas onto ships at local Windward ports for sale to the joint venture company WIBDECO/FYFFES based in the United Kingdom. WIBDECO also conducts research, provides technical assistance to BGAs, and inspects banana fields for quality control.

Table 10. ECCB Area: Rate of Growth of Gross Domestic Product by Economic Activity, at Factor Cost, in Constant Prices[1]
(Percent)

Sector	Average 1977–89	1990	1991	1992	1993	1994	1995	1996	1997	1998
Total	6.0	4.7	0.7	3.9	2.6	3.0	0.7	2.7	3.1	2.3
Agriculture	2.1	6.4	–7.7	9.5	–1.0	–13.5	5.0	–0.6	–7.7	–6.6
Crops	2.7	7.7	–10.7	11.1	–2.1	–18.6	7.8	–1.6	–11.9	–11.6
Livestock	1.9	8.1	–2.2	3.1	–1.4	3.0	–3.5	4.2	1.3	5.3
Forestry	–1.5	0.2	–0.1	0.9	–0.4	–0.9	–0.8	–1.0	–3.4	0.3
Fishing	1.2	–1.2	6.7	6.0	5.0	2.4	–1.2	1.2	5.9	4.8
Mining and quarrying	14.3	–9.8	5.9	2.7	–2.9	–0.6	7.8	3.8	6.9	–5.9
Manufacturing	7.7	0.0	–1.5	4.9	–3.0	–1.2	3.8	2.3	1.9	–3.7
Electricity and water	7.2	7.7	4.7	10.5	–0.3	7.6	4.6	4.6	6.3	8.0
Construction	10.5	2.0	–5.7	3.2	–1.7	3.8	5.1	2.9	7.1	3.7
Wholesale and retail trade	5.5	9.5	2.1	3.0	2.6	2.1	1.7	2.2	3.7	3.2
Hotels and restaurants	8.9	5.6	4.7	8.5	6.7	15.2	–11.3	3.4	7.3	0.6
Transport	7.6	5.3	–1.1	0.5	4.9	5.1	–0.1	3.9	5.4	4.0
Road transport	7.1	5.6	1.8	0.0	3.3	4.3	0.6	2.9	7.3	3.7
Sea transport	8.8	4.7	–10.0	–0.6	6.6	5.7	1.4	7.9	0.7	11.7
Air transport	7.9	5.1	1.1	3.5	8.3	7.0	–3.6	2.2	5.1	–4.2
Communications	15.7	15.9	16.7	3.7	7.8	12.8	5.2	6.2	5.4	2.7
Banks and insurance	8.9	6.0	4.5	4.5	6.8	5.4	6.1	6.8	9.1	3.9
Real estate and housing	2.6	2.1	3.7	1.9	2.0	2.0	–4.0	–0.1	1.7	2.4
Government services	4.8	2.0	2.1	–0.5	1.6	3.3	1.2	1.8	1.9	4.7
Other services	4.8	8.9	2.3	2.2	9.9	2.5	0.2	1.8	0.6	2.6
Less imputed service charges	8.5	13.6	7.2	2.1	4.8	7.8	9.4	5.8	10.2	2.3

Source: Eastern Caribbean Central Bank.
[1] The area includes Anguilla, Antigua and Barbuda, Dominica, Grenada, Montserrat, St. Kitts and Nevis, St. Lucia, and St. Vincent and the Grenadines.

1997, almost one third of the farmers in Dominica and St. Lucia, and 17 percent of banana farmers in St. Vincent and the Grenadines had been certified, and the Windward Islands' score on the quality index for exported bananas had improved to 84 from 76 in 1996 (on a scale of 100, with a score of 80 or more generally considered acceptable). At the same time, efforts were undertaken to reduce production and marketing costs through the introduction of a new carton-purchasing system, usage of pallets (as opposed to boxes) in shipping, and irrigation projects (especially in St. Vincent and the Grenadines). In part due to these efforts, output increased somewhat in 1998 (St. Vincent and the Grenadines registered an increase of about 30 percent).

Tourism

Tourism, as noted, has become an increasingly important sector in the economies of the ECCB region. The number of stayover arrivals[30] increased at an average annual rate of nearly 4 percent during 1990–98 (Tables 19 and 20), while the number of hotel rooms expanded at an average annual rate of 15 percent (Table 21), and employment almost doubled to over 14,500. St. Lucia registered the fastest growth in stayover arrivals during the period (average annual growth rate of about 8 percent), followed by Dominica (around 5 percent). In contrast, stay-

---
[30] Visitors staying at least one night.

IV RECENT ECONOMIC DEVELOPMENTS

Table 11. ECCB Area: Contribution of Gross Domestic Product by Economic Activity, at Factor Cost, in Current Prices[1]
(Percent)

Sector	Average 1977–89	1990	1991	1992	1993	1994	1995	1996	1997	1998
Total	100.0	100.0	100.0	100.0	100.0	100.0	100.0	100.0	100.0	100.0
Agriculture	15.2	12.2	11.5	11.6	10.1	9.0	9.3	8.7	8.1	8.2
Crops	11.4	9.5	8.7	8.8	7.3	6.3	6.6	6.0	5.4	5.5
Livestock	1.5	1.0	0.9	0.9	0.9	0.9	0.8	0.8	0.8	0.8
Forestry	0.6	0.3	0.3	0.3	0.3	0.3	0.3	0.3	0.3	0.3
Fishing	1.7	1.4	1.5	1.5	1.6	1.5	1.5	1.5	1.6	1.6
Mining and quarrying	0.7	0.8	0.8	0.8	0.8	0.7	0.8	0.8	0.8	0.8
Manufacturing	7.5	6.7	6.7	6.7	6.3	5.9	6.2	6.1	5.9	5.7
Electricity and water	2.6	3.1	3.4	3.7	3.8	4.1	3.9	3.8	4.0	4.1
Construction	8.6	10.5	9.8	9.7	9.5	9.4	9.7	9.7	10.0	10.7
Wholesale and retail trade	12.6	12.3	12.6	12.6	12.6	12.4	12.6	12.6	12.6	12.7
Hotels and restaurants	7.3	8.9	9.1	9.5	9.8	11.0	10.0	10.2	10.4	10.1
Transport	10.7	11.2	11.2	11.1	11.4	11.3	11.3	11.5	11.8	11.5
Road transport	6.6	6.5	6.5	6.4	6.6	6.5	6.5	6.6	6.7	6.5
Sea transport	2.3	2.7	2.6	2.6	2.6	2.5	2.6	2.7	2.7	2.6
Air transport	1.8	2.0	2.1	2.1	2.2	2.3	2.2	2.3	2.4	2.3
Communications	4.1	6.4	7.0	6.7	7.1	7.6	7.7	7.8	7.8	7.7
Banks and insurance	6.6	8.0	8.0	8.0	8.8	9.0	9.3	9.5	9.7	9.9
Real estate and housing	7.4	5.8	5.7	5.7	5.6	5.4	5.1	5.0	4.9	4.7
Government services	16.9	16.2	16.2	15.9	16.2	16.7	17.0	17.1	17.2	17.3
Other services	4.6	4.0	4.0	4.0	4.4	4.4	4.5	4.5	4.4	4.3
Less imputed service charges	4.7	6.2	6.2	6.0	6.4	6.8	7.3	7.3	7.6	7.6

Sources: Eastern Caribbean Central Bank, and IMF staff estimates.
[1] The area includes Anguilla, Antigua and Barbuda, Dominica, Grenada, Montserrat, St. Kitts and Nevis, St. Lucia, and St. Vincent and the Grenadines.

over arrivals in Antigua and Barbuda grew at an average rate of only 1½ percent a year during the same period. As a result, by 1995 St. Lucia had become the number one destination, replacing Antigua and Barbuda.

The Caribbean is the most important destination in the world for the cruise industry, accounting for more than 50 percent of world cruise ship passengers. Cruise tourism expanded rapidly in the ECCB region as well as in the rest of the Caribbean during the 1990s (Table 22). In particular, cruise ship tourist arrivals increased at an annual average rate of 10½ percent during 1990–98 in the ECCB region. Dominica had the largest annual average increase in cruise ship tourist arrivals (56 percent) during this period (from a very low base), followed by St. Kitts and Nevis and St. Lucia (21 percent and 18 percent). In contrast, the number of cruise ship tourist arrivals to St. Vincent and the Grenadines declined sharply.

Reflecting the increase in total arrivals, tourism earnings of the ECCB region increased at an average annual rate of about 6 percent during 1990–98 (Table 23). St. Vincent and the Grenadines had the highest average annual growth rate of receipts from tourism, followed by St. Lucia and Dominica. Nevertheless, and despite the 1995 hurricanes, Antigua and Barbuda continued to be one of the two largest recipients of tourism earnings (along with St. Lucia), reflecting its concentration in the high end of the market. The share of the ECCB region in the total tourism receipts of the Caribbean has remained in the range of 6–7 percent, performance that was due in part to the large proportion of visitors who arrive

Table 12. ECBB Area: Saving and Investment
(Percent of GDP)

	1990	1991	1992	1993	1994	1995	1996	1997	1998
Gross national saving	16.7	14.2	16.7	18.8	17.8	22.2	17.5	15.9	15.3
Antigua and Barbuda	19.6	17.6	16.9	25.5	21.3	39.3	23.7	19.1	15.9
Dominica	14.5	12.6	16.3	15.7	9.0	12.1	9.4	10.7	17.2
Grenada	18.8	21.6	21.4	17.0	25.8	17.0	16.5	16.1	13.6
St. Kitts and Nevis	26.2	21.1	30.2	30.1	27.3	25.7	17.3	24.8	30.0
St. Lucia	11.8	9.2	13.0	14.9	15.9	14.0	11.7	10.8	8.6
St. Vincent and the Grenadines	18.8	9.5	16.3	12.1	8.6	17.8	21.2	15.7	16.9
Gross domestic investment	33.6	30.8	27.3	29.4	28.8	31.9	31.9	32.0	31.2
Antigua and Barbuda	27.5	25.8	21.4	25.6	24.9	39.4	36.8	30.2	31.5
Dominica	40.8	31.6	29.5	27.0	26.8	32.6	26.3	24.5	24.3
Grenada	39.7	40.7	34.2	34.4	36.2	31.9	36.1	38.1	40.6
St. Kitts and Nevis	56.2	42.9	38.7	44.9	37.8	45.2	45.1	44.9	45.4
St. Lucia	25.8	25.3	24.1	24.8	23.9	18.7	21.4	24.6	19.3
St. Vincent and the Grenadines	31.1	30.8	26.6	30.5	32.5	33.3	32.5	37.5	36.7
External current account	−16.9	−16.6	−10.6	−10.7	−11.0	−9.7	−14.4	−16.0	−15.8
Antigua and Barbuda	−7.9	−8.2	−4.5	−0.1	−3.6	−0.1	−13.1	−11.1	−15.6
Dominica	−26.3	−19.0	−13.2	−11.3	−17.8	−20.5	−16.9	−13.8	−7.1
Grenada	−20.8	−19.1	−12.8	−17.4	−10.4	−14.9	−19.6	−22.0	−27.0
St. Kitts and Nevis	−30.0	−21.9	−8.5	−14.8	−10.5	−19.5	−27.8	−20.1	−15.4
St. Lucia	−14.0	−16.1	−11.1	−10.0	−8.0	−4.7	−9.7	−13.8	−10.7
St. Vincent and the Grenadines	−12.3	−21.3	−10.3	−18.4	−23.9	−15.4	−11.3	−21.7	−19.8

Sources: Eastern Caribbean Central Bank, and IMF staff estimates.

Table 13. ECCB Area: Consumer Prices
(Annual percentage change)

	1990	1991	1992	1993	1994	1995	1996	1997	1998
					End of period				
ECCB Area	5.1	4.3	3.6	2.5	2.2	2.1	2.1	2.6	3.1
Antigua and Barbuda	7.7	1.5	3.0	3.1	3.8	−1.3	3.2	−1.1	4.7
Dominica	3.1	5.6	5.3	1.6	0.0	1.4	2.0	2.2	2.0
Grenada	3.7	1.0	4.6	3.5	1.9	2.1	3.1	0.9	1.4
St. Kitts and Nevis	3.7	4.6	1.5	1.4	1.3	2.6	3.1	11.3	3.6
St. Lucia	5.2	7.2	3.5	0.7	5.9	4.6	−2.3	1.6	3.6
St. Vincent and the Grenadines	7.2	5.9	3.8	4.5	0.4	3.1	3.6	0.8	3.3
					Period average				
ECCB Area	4.5	5.0	4.1	2.3	2.0	2.7	3.6	1.4	2.5
Antigua and Barbuda	6.9	5.8	3.0	3.1	3.5	2.5	3.0	0.3	3.4
Dominica	2.0	5.5	5.3	1.6	0.0	1.3	1.7	2.4	0.9
Grenada	2.7	2.6	3.8	2.8	2.6	2.2	2.8	1.3	1.4
St. Kitts and Nevis	4.2	4.2	2.9	1.4	3.0	2.0	8.9	3.6	4.1
St. Lucia	3.8	6.1	5.7	0.8	2.7	5.9	0.9	0.0	2.8
St. Vincent and the Grenadines	7.3	5.9	3.8	4.3	0.4	2.3	4.4	0.5	2.1
Memorandum items:									
United States (end of period)	6.1	3.1	2.9	2.7	2.7	2.5	3.3	1.7	1.6
United States (period average)	5.4	4.2	3.0	2.9	2.6	2.8	2.9	2.3	1.5

Sources: Eastern Caribbean Central Bank.

IV RECENT ECONOMIC DEVELOPMENTS

Table 14. Windward Islands: Selected Banana Sector Indicators

	1990	1991	1992	1993	1994	1995	1996	1997	1998
Exports (tons)	281,941	227,061	279,800	242,450	169,385	193,644	191,408	137,428	144,671
Dominica	57,867	55,847	59,221	55,940	43,205	33,368	39,957	34,911	29,150
St. Lucia	135,367	100,877	135,291	122,930	90,713	105,633	105,547	71,395	74,666
St. Vincent and the Grenadines	81,155	63,411	78,777	58,689	30,925	50,084	44,038	31,020	40,761
Grenada	7,552	6,926	6,511	4,891	4,542	4,559	1,866	102	94
Exports (EC$ million)	386.8	326.7	376.4	269.9	217.4	207.2	224.4	164.8	188.8
Dominica	79.6	80.9	82.4	65.1	55.4	45.2	44.5	41.7	37.8
St. Lucia	186.9	146.4	184.8	137.9	115.7	115.7	125.8	85.9	94.2
St. Vincent and the Grenadines	110.0	89.5	101.4	62.0	39.8	39.8	52.4	37.1	56.9
Grenada	10.3	9.9	7.8	4.8	6.5	6.5	1.6	…	…
Share of banana exports in ECCB area merchandise exports (percent)	41.8	37.5	38.5	30.4	29.7	24.1	27.6	23.2	24.5
Memorandum items:									
Average green market price (£/ton)									
For Windward Islands bananas	525.0	579.0	538.0	541.0	618.0	548.0	544.0	548.0	564.0
For dollar bananas	…	542.0	534.7	581.0	659.0	622.0	603.0	601.0	587.0
Average exchange rate (EC$/£)	4.8	4.8	4.7	4.0	4.1	4.3	4.2	4.4	4.4

Sources: Windward Island Banana Development and Export Company (WIBDECO).

aboard cruise ships, as spending by these visitors is comparatively small.

Public Finances

Most of the ECCB member countries maintained fairly sound fiscal policies in the 1990s, but there were noticeable differences in performance. St. Lucia and St. Vincent and the Grenadines attained substantial public saving and moderate public sector surpluses or relatively small deficits during most of the period, while Antigua and Barbuda showed persistent negative public saving and a public sector deficit averaging 5 percent of GDP over 1990–98 (Table 24). In Dominica and Grenada, countries that undertook largely successful adjustment efforts in the 1980s with IMF support, performance has been unsteady, with public sector balances deteriorating in 1997–98, although in Grenada the public sector deficit narrowed in 1999. In the case of St. Kitts and Nevis, the condition of the public finances weakened markedly in 1998, mainly as a result of the damage inflicted by Hurricane Georges, and again in 1999 when reconstruction got under way.

While the consolidated public sector deficit of the region was generally small in the 1990s, there was a noticeable increase in 1997–98 (Table 25) that appears to have persisted in 1999. This weakening was associated mostly with a deterioration in the finances of the central governments (Table 26), as the rest of the public sector has continued to register small surpluses, largely because of the strong financial position of the social security agencies. The surpluses of these agencies reflect the comparatively small number of pensioners. The rest of the public sector includes local governments, which have remained dependent on central government transfers; public enterprises, the number of which has continued to be reduced through privatization; and export boards (mainly involved in the banana business), which have required substantial transfers from central governments because of competitiveness problems.

The consolidated overall balance of the central governments showed deficits that averaged 2⅔ percent of GDP a year over the period 1990–98 (Table 27). The deficits increased markedly in 1997–98, reaching an estimated 4 percent of GDP in 1998. While the hurricane damage in St. Kitts and Nevis and in Antigua and Barbuda in 1998 played a role in this increase, there also has been a tendency for current spending to rise since 1991.

Government saving fell from an average of 2 percent of GDP in 1990–96 to 1 percent of GDP in 1997, and further to around ⅓ percent of GDP in 1998. This was largely the result of the growing rise in current expenditure that began in 1994. While this tendency was evident throughout the region, it was most pronounced in St. Kitts and Nevis, where gov-

Box 5. The EU Banana Regime

The Windward Islands (Dominica, Grenada, St. Lucia, and St. Vincent and the Grenadines) have been exporting bananas to the United Kingdom since 1953. From the beginning, these exports have been critically dependent on preferential duty-free access. Until 1993, France and Italy had similar arrangements for their ex-colonies; Germany imported all bananas duty free; Ireland, Denmark, Belgium, and the Netherlands imposed a common external tariff of 20 percent and imported bananas almost exclusively from Latin America ("dollar bananas"); and Spain was supplied domestically from the Canary Islands and effectively prohibited banana imports. These arrangements ended in 1993 when the unified European Union (EU) banana regime began. The main features of the regime that was applied until December 31, 1998 included:

- A system of country-specific banana allocations for the 12 African, Caribbean, and Pacific countries (ACP)[1] that had traditionally supplied the EC market. These bananas were imported duty free and the total of these allocations was 857,000 tons annually (Tables 15 and 16).
- A basic tariff quota of 2.2 million tons for nontraditional ACP bananas and third-country bananas. Nontraditional ACP bananas were defined as both any excess over traditional quantities (above their individual country ceiling) supplied by traditional ACP countries and any quantities supplied by those ACP countries not considered traditional suppliers to the EU, such as the Dominican Republic. Third-country bananas were all other, including Latin American, bananas. In addition, a supplementary quota of 353,000 tons annually was introduced in 1995 to accommodate the expansion of EU membership incorporating Austria, Finland, and Sweden. Out of the total quota of 2.553 million tons, the nontraditional ACP bananas were reserved a share of 90,000 tons, divided into country-specific allocations. The tariff rate was zero for this 90,000 tons of nontraditional ACP bananas, ECU 75 per ton for third-country bananas, ECU 693 per ton for any nontraditional ACP bananas above 90,000 tons, and ECU 765 per ton for any third-country bananas above the 2.553 million ton quota.
- An import licensing system under which importers of bananas from EU territories or traditional ACP countries were entitled to 30 percent of the licenses for the importation of the 2.553 million tons mentioned above.[2]
- A system of financial support and restructuring schemes for bananas produced within the EU territories (including Guadeloupe, Martinique, Canary Islands, and Madeira).

From the beginning this EU banana regime was controversial with Latin American banana producers and with some EU countries, such as Germany, Belgium, and the Netherlands, and thus was subject to several legal challenges at the GATT as well as at the European Court of Justice. The last challenge was launched by four Latin American banana-exporting countries, (Mexico, Honduras, Guatemala, and Ecuador) and the United States. These countries filed a joint complaint against the EU at the WTO in September 1995.

In May 1997 the WTO Dispute Settlement Panel ruled that some aspects of the current EU banana regime, including the licensing system, are inconsistent with the WTO rules. The EU promptly appealed against the ruling. However, the Appellate Board of the WTO upheld the ruling in September 1997 and the European Union was given until January 1, 1999 to change its import regime.

In response, on July 20, 1998, the EU issued a new council regulation (1637/98) with the expectation of satisfying the WTO ruling. The main features of the regulation are: (i) a global duty-free allocation of 857,700 tons annually for traditional ACP banana producers; (ii) a tariff quota of 2.2 million tons annually at the reduced duty of ECU 75 per ton for third-country bananas and tariff-free for nontraditional ACP bananas; (iii) an additional quota of 0.353 million tons annually with a duty of ECU 75 per ton applicable beyond the above bound tariff quota for third-country bananas and tariff-free for non-traditional ACP bananas; (iv) a reduction of ECU 200 in the tariff for nontraditional ACP bananas beyond the quota; (v) a proposed system for subdividing the tariff quota and, if the situation arises, the traditional ACP quantity, using a single criterion for determining those producer states with a substantial interest in the supply of bananas; and (vi) a single license system for bananas of any origin.

Nevertheless, the WTO dispute panel issued a report on April 12, 1999 finding that the EU banana quota and licensing system discriminated against U.S. marketing companies and Latin American suppliers. However, it stated that the EU could still grant preferential duty-free entry to bananas from the ACP countries under the Lome Convention, which benefits from a WTO rule waiver.

A subsequent EU proposal to reform its banana regime (announced by the European Commission on November 10, 1999) has been opposed by the United States and Latin American producers. The proposal aims at the abolition of import quotas by January 1, 2006, following an interim period involving a system of quotas subject to tariffs, in which bananas from ACP countries would pay a preferential tariff.

---

[1] The traditional ACP countries in the Caribbean are Belize, Jamaica, Suriname and the Windward Islands.

[2] The so-called "Category B" operators, defined as those who have marketed bananas from the EU territories and/or traditional ACP countries, were entitled to licenses to import 30 percent of the 2.553 million ton quota. The allocation of 30 percent among the Category B operators was based on a complicated formula. A Category B operator could sell its licenses to any other operator.

IV RECENT ECONOMIC DEVELOPMENTS

Table 15. EU: Duty-Free Banana Import Quotas for ACP Countries

	Traditional Quantities (Tons)	Nontraditional Quantities (Tons)
Total	857,700	90,000
Caribbean ACP countries		
Traditional		
Belize	40,000	15,000
Dominica	71,000	
Grenada	14,000	
Jamaica	105,000	
St. Lucia	127,000	
St. Vincent and the Grenadines	82,000	
Suriname	38,000	
Nontraditional		
Dominican Republic		55,000
Subtotal	477,000	
Other ACP countries		
Traditional		
Cameroon	155,000	7,500
Cape Verde	4,800	
Ivory Coast	155,000	7,500
Madagascar	5,900	
Somalia	60,000	
Nontraditional		
Others		5,000
Subtotal	380,700	

Source: European Union Council Regulation 404/93.

ernment current expenditure rose from an average of 25 percent of GDP in 1990–96 to 30½ percent of GDP in 1997–98 (Table 28). The rise in current expenditure took place in both government wage bills and spending on goods and services, and it also reflected higher interest obligations, reducing the scope for short-term flexibility in fiscal policy. For the region as a whole, government wage and interest obligations stood at 15 percent of GDP in 1997–98, or the equivalent of 70 percent of tax revenue. In the cases of Antigua and Barbuda, Dominica, and St. Kitts and Nevis, these obligations amounted to the equivalent of 77–80 percent of tax revenue in 1997–98.[31]

---

[31]Governments in Antigua and Barbuda (1994), St. Kitts (1995), and St. Lucia (1997) instituted short-term public employment schemes aimed at alleviating unemployment. Also, it is worth noting that the Government of Grenada has been transferring certain health and other services and staff to newly created statutory boards. While this has reduced the central government wage bill, central government transfers to the rest of the public sector have increased.

After growing faster than GDP over 1990–96, government current revenue stayed at 25 percent of GDP in 1997–98. The upward trend in the ratio of government current revenue to GDP registered during most of the 1990s arose mainly from a marked increase in nontax current revenue associated largely with the relative success of efforts to promote offshore businesses in some countries, most notably in St. Kitts and Nevis and Dominica.[32] Tax revenue was broadly stable at a little over 21 percent of GDP during the 1990s. Revenue from taxes on goods and services averaged about 9½ percent of GDP, remaining the largest source of government revenue, followed by collections from taxes on international trade. A high proportion of the collections on domestic transactions, however, is actually derived from the levying of consumption taxes on imports. Despite the virtual elimination of the personal income tax in Grenada in 1996, income tax collections in the region remained largely unchanged subsequently at about 5 percent of GDP, as the fall in collections in Grenada coincided with improvements in St. Kitts and Nevis and in St. Vincent and the Grenadines.

While the average tax ratio in the region is high relative to other countries in the Western Hemisphere, there are important differences across countries. Dominica and St. Vincent and the Grenadines have maintained the strongest tax effort, with tax ratios that averaged nearly 24 percent of GDP in 1990–98, whereas Antigua and Barbuda exhibited the lowest effort with an average tax ratio of close to 18 percent of GDP (Table 29). Differences are sharp in income tax collections, which averaged 7 percent of GDP in St. Vincent and the Grenadines and only 2 percent of GDP in Antigua and Barbuda, where there is no personal income tax.[33] The contrast is also marked in taxes on goods and services, as collections averaged 12 percent of GDP in Dominica and Grenada and only 8 percent of GDP in Antigua and Barbuda. Similarly, dependence on taxes on international trade and transactions has been highest in Antigua and Barbuda, and St. Kitts and Nevis where it averaged about 7–7½ percent of GDP in 1990–98, whereas in Dominica and St. Vincent and the Grenadines, it only brought in the equivalent of around 4½ percent of GDP.

In spite of the regional trade liberalization that began in 1993, collections from taxes on international trade and transactions remained broadly unchanged in most countries (see Table 29). There has

---

[32]Antigua and Barbuda has remained by far the largest offshore center in the region; its system was described in IMF Staff Country Report No. 98/7, *Antigua and Barbuda: Recent Economic Developments*.

[33]For details on taxes in the OECS countries, see IMF Staff Country Report No. 99/36, *Grenada: Statistical Annex* (Table 28).

Public Finances

Table 16. EU: Comparison of Quota/Tariff Structure Under the Previous and Current Banana Import Regimes

	Quota (Tons)		Tariff Rate (ECU Per Ton)	
Previous EU Banana Import Regime				
Traditional ACP bananas[1]	857,700 (the sum of country-specific quotas)		Within quota[2]	0
Nontraditional ACP bananas[3]	2,200,000 (basic) plus 353,000 (supplementary)	Reserved share of 90,000 (the sum of country-specific quotas)	Within quota Outside of quota	0 693
Third country bananas[4]		The rest	Within quota Outside of quota	75 765
Current New EU Banana Import Regime				
Traditional ACP bananas	857,7000 (no country-specific quotas)			0
	Basic Quota	Additional Quota		Basic and Additional Quota
Nontraditional ACP bananas	2,200,000	353,000	Within quota Outside of quota	0 565
Third country Bananas			Within quota Outside of quota	75 765

Source: European Union Council Regulations 404/93 and 1637/98.
[1] Defined as the bananas from 12 specific ACP countries (the traditional ACP countries) within a country-specific quota.
[2] By definition, any amount outside of a country-specific quota falls into the category of "nontraditional ACP bananas."
[3] Defined as both any quantities in excess of traditional quantities supplied by traditional ACP countries and any quantities supplied by nontraditional ACP countries.
[4] Defined as all other bananas.

Table 17. Windward Islands: Banana Growers Profile[1]

Grower Profile	I	II	III	IV	V
Area cultivated in each group (percent)	1.4	11.5	19.5	44.5	23.1
Yield (ton/acre)	12.5	9.5	7.2	4.6	3.4
Average plot area (acre)	9.0	7.3	4.6	2.7	1.3
Cost of production (EC¢ per pound)	30.0	37.0	41.0	66.0	68.0

Source: Windward Islands Banana Industry-Production Recovery Plan, July 1998.
[1] Windward Islands banana growers are classified in five groups according to their productivity (output per acre).

been some decline in average import duty rates and duty collections relative to GDP (Table 30) as a result of the implementation of reductions in the common external tariff (CET) under the CARICOM Agreement. This was offset by improvements in collections from other taxes levied on imports (mainly customs service charges), visitors, and foreign exchange transactions.

Public sector investment in the region averaged about 8 percent of GDP over the period 1990–98, and public saving helped fund about half of it (see Table 25). Most of the public sector investment (around three-fourths) has been undertaken by the central governments, with the remainder implemented by the public enterprises. In 1997–98, due to a decline in public saving and a rise in public invest-

IV RECENT ECONOMIC DEVELOPMENTS

Table 18. Windward Islands: Banana Recovery Plan[1]

Year ending:	1998	1999	2000	2001
Dominica				
Acres cultivated	8,826	7,500	7,250	7,000
Number of farmers	3,000	2,500	2,300	2,100
Tons	31,577	43,583	49,000	54,000
Yield (tons/acres)	3.6	5.8	6.8	7.7
St. Lucia				
Acres cultivated	13,250	13,261	13,274	13,287
Number of farmers	3,679	2,247	2,250	2,250
Tons	71,000	90,000	100,000	110,000
Yield (tons/acres)	5.4	6.8	7.5	8.3
St. Vincent and the Grenadines				
Acres cultivated	5,992	6,496	7,000	7,000
Number of farmers	3,374	3,132	2,900	2,900
Tons	32,000	48,181	54,349	65,527
Yield (tons/acre)	5.3	7.4	7.8	9.4

Source: Windward Islands Banana Industry-Production Recovery Plan, July 1998.
[1]Production levels expected to reduce the dead freight cost and help sustain the guaranteed price to farmers as envisaged in the Banana Recovery Plan.

Table 19. Caribbean Region: Stayover Tourist Arrivals
(In thousands, unless otherwise indicated)

	1990	1991	1992	1993	1994	1995	1996	1997	1998
Caribbean total	11,731.2	11,927.9	12,301.4	13,359.0	14,254.5	14,489.6	14,904.8	15,859.1	16,449.8
ECCB Area	650.7	679.4	719.1	793.3	861.2	816.1	823.7	866.6	879.6
Anguilla	31.2	29.7	30.4	37.7	43.7	38.5	37.5	43.2	43.9
Antigua and Barbuda	205.7	204.7	217.9	249.4	262.9	220.0	228.2	240.4	234.3
Dominica	45.1	46.3	47.0	51.9	56.5	60.5	63.3	65.4	65.5
Grenada	82.0	85.0	87.6	93.9	109.0	108.0	108.2	110.7	115.8
Montserrat	18.7	19.2	17.3	21.0	21.3	17.7	8.7	5.1	7.5
St. Kitts and Nevis	75.7	83.9	88.3	88.6	94.2	78.9	84.2	88.3	93.2
St. Lucia	138.4	159.0	177.5	194.1	218.6	232.3	235.7	248.4	252.2
St. Vincent and the Grenadines	53.9	51.6	53.1	56.7	55.0	60.2	57.9	65.1	67.2
Other Caribbean countries	11,080.5	11,248.5	11,582.3	12,565.7	13,393.3	13,673.5	14,081.1	14,992.5	15,570.2
Bahamas	1,561.6	1,427.0	1,398.9	1,488.7	1,516.0	1,598.1	1,633.1	1,617.6	1,540.0
Cuba	340.3	424.0	460.6	544.1	617.3	762.7	1,004.3	1,170.1	1,415.8
Dominican Republic	1,530.0	1,416.8	1,523.8	1,636.4	1,766.9	1,775.9	1,925.6	2,211.4	2,309.1
Jamaica	840.8	1,006.8	1,057.2	1,105.4	1,098.3	1,147.0	1,162.4	1,192.2	1,225.3
Puerto Rico	2,559.7	2,613.0	2,753.9	2,923.2	3,112.7	3,053.9	3,127.7	3,378.5	3,461.3
Others[1]	4,248.1	4,360.9	4,387.9	4,867.9	5,282.1	5,335.9	5,228.0	5,422.7	5,618.7
Memorandum items:									
Share of ECCB in Caribbean (in percent)	5.5	5.7	5.8	5.9	6.0	5.6	5.5	5.5	5.3
World total (in millions)	458.2	464.0	502.8	518.3	553.3	568.5	599.6	619.6	635.1
Share of ECCB in world total (in percent)	0.14	0.15	0.14	0.15	0.16	0.14	0.14	0.14	0.14

Sources: Caribbean Tourism Organization, World Tourism Organization.
[1]Includes Barbados, Belize, Bermuda, Cayman Islands, Guyana, Trinidad and Tobago, Turks and Caicos Islands, Aruba, Bonaire, Curaçao, Saba, St. Eustatius, St. Maarten, Guadeloupe, Martinique, Haiti, Suriname, and U.S. Virgin Islands.

Public Finances

Table 20. ECCB Area: Stayover Tourist Arrivals by Country of Origin
(Thousands)

	1990	1991	1992	1993	1994	1995	1996	1997	1998
Total	650.7	679.4	719.1	793.3	861.2	816.1	823.7	866.6	879.6
United States	217.7	216.6	225.2	268.8	293.3	276.9	258.7	267.5	278.4
Canada	55.0	49.4	50.9	50.8	55.0	45.1	49.0	56.6	51.1
Europe	155.7	173.3	201.8	226.8	257.5	236.3	247.0	265.6	260.5
United Kingdom	90.6	93.7	115.0	136.0	155.7	141.6	146.8	167.2	178.5
Germany[1]	26.3	29.3	33.3	35.8	41.0	32.8	32.9	27.9	22.9
France[1]	12.9	14.4	16.7	17.0	17.5	17.9	24.6	27.7	20.3
Others	25.8	35.9	36.8	38.0	43.3	44.0	42.7	42.7	38.8
Caribbean	160.5	173.8	176.1	178.9	192.0	199.1	209.1	213.2	222.0
Others	61.8	66.3	65.1	68.0	63.4	58.7	59.9	63.7	67.6
Memorandum items:									
Tourist arrivals in total									
Caribbean (in percent)									
From the United States	55.8	53.7	52.4	54.2	53.0	50.8	49.6	48.5	47.8
From Europe	14.0	15.7	16.6	20.4	23.7	24.8	26.3	27.2	27.9

Source: Caribbean Tourism Organization.
[1] Data estimated for 1990.

Table 21. Caribbean Region: Number of Hotel Rooms[1]

	1990	1991	1992	1993	1994	1995	1996	1997	1998
Caribbean total	83,774	140,785	150,346	161,210	166,740	174,969	184,315	194,137	205,342
ECCB Area	4,687	10,955	11,817	12,939	12,952	13,931	13,331	13,383	13,937
Anguilla	150	863	920	978	978	951	866	915	1,045
Antigua and Barbuda	1,350	2,752	3,317	3,317	3,317	3,317	3,185	3,185	3,185
Dominica	157	547	603	757	757	588	764	824	824
Grenada	570	1,118	1,114	1,428	1,428	1,652	1,669	1,775	1,802
Montserrat	131	710	710	710	710	710	...	...	...
St. Kitts and Nevis	584	1,392	1,330	1,600	1,593	1,563	1,610	1,729	1,762
St. Lucia	1,245	2,464	2,659	2,919	2,954	3,974	3,986	3,701	3,769
St. Vincent and the Grenadines	500	1,109	1,164	1,230	1,215	1,176	1,251	1,254	1,550
Other Caribbean countries	79,087	129,830	138,529	148,271	153,788	161,038	170,984	180,754	191,405
Bahamas	11,429	13,165	13,541	13,521	13,398	13,421	13,288	13,288	14,243
Cuba	7,526	16,638	18,682	22,561	23,254	24,233	26,878	31,837	35,708
Dominican Republic	3,800	22,555	24,410	26,801	28,967	32,475	35,729	38,250	42,412
Jamaica	10,092	17,337	18,489	18,935	19,760	20,896	21,984	22,954	22,713
Puerto Rico	9,224	7,897	8,415	8,581	9,519	10,251	10,245	10,849	11,828
Others[2]	37,016	52,238	54,992	57,872	58,890	59,762	62,860	63,576	64,501
Memorandum item:									
Share of ECCB in total Caribbean (in percent)	5.6	7.8	7.9	8.0	7.8	8.0	7.2	6.9	6.8

Source: Caribbean Tourism Organization.
[1] Includes apartments, villas, and guest houses.
[2] Includes Barbados, Belize, Bermuda, Cayman Islands, Guyana, Trinidad and Tobago, Turks and Caicos Islands, Aruba, Bonaire, Curaçao, Saba, St. Eustatius, St. Maarten, Guadeloupe, Martinique, Haiti, Suriname, and U.S. Virgin Islands.

IV RECENT ECONOMIC DEVELOPMENTS

Table 22. Caribbean Region: Cruise Passenger Arrivals
(Thousands)

	1990	1991	1992	1993	1994	1995	1996	1997	1998
Caribbean total	7,393.7	8,176.4	8,758.6	8,866.3	8,852.5	8,757.5	9,687.3	10,769.5	10,899.4
ECCB Area	631.7	809.9	843.8	841.9	927.9	1,003.3	1,060.5	1,206.3	1,398.2
Antigua and Barbuda	227.3	255.6	250.2	238.4	235.7	227.4	270.5	285.5	336.2
Dominica	6.8	65.0	89.8	87.8	125.5	134.9	193.5	229.9	236.1
Grenada	183.2	196.1	195.9	200.1	200.8	249.9	267.0	246.6	265.9
Montserrat	...	...	5.6	8.8	11.0	9.0	...	...	...
St. Kitts and Nevis	33.9	52.8	74.0	83.1	112.9	120.9	85.8	102.7	154.1
St. Lucia	101.9	152.8	164.9	154.4	171.5	175.9	180.5	310.2	372.1
St. Vincent and the Grenadines	78.6	87.6	63.4	69.3	70.5	85.3	63.2	31.4	33.8
Other Caribbean countries	6,762.0	7,366.5	7,914.8	8,024.4	7,924.6	7,754.2	8,626.8	9,563.2	9,501.2
Bahamas	1,853.9	2,020.0	2,139.4	2,047.0	1,805.6	1,543.5	1,687.1	1,751.1	1,729.9
Dominican Republic	50.0	50.0	50.0	27.8	50.1	30.5	110.9	270.8	393.6
Jamaica	385.8	490.5	649.5	629.6	595.0	605.2	658.2	711.7	673.7
Puerto Rico	892.9	994.9	1,019.2	968.1	976.9	1,001.1	1,025.1	1,227.4	1,243.4
Others[1]	3,579.4	3,811.1	4,056.7	4,351.9	4,497.0	4,573.9	5,145.5	5,602.2	5,460.6
Memorandum items:									
Share of ECCB in total Caribbean (in percent)	8.5	9.9	9.6	9.5	10.5	11.5	10.9	11.2	12.8

Source: Caribbean Tourism Organization.
[1] Includes Barbados, Belize, Bermuda, Cayman Islands, Trinidad and Tobago, Aruba, Bonaire, Curaçao, St. Maarten, Guadeloupe, Martinique, and U.S. Virgin Islands.

Table 23. Caribbean Region: Visitor Expenditure
(Millions of U.S. dollars)

	1990	1991	1992	1993	1994	1995	1996	1997	1998
Caribbean total	8,841.8	9,068.7	9,855.2	10,943.4	11,763.1	12,590.8	13,474.3	14,291.9	15,058.3
ECCB Area	542.4	585.8	652.0	728.2	807.9	770.1	799.8	859.4	873.4
Anguilla	36.0	39.1	39.6	48.9	56.3	50.3	50.8	60.4	61.7
Antigua and Barbuda	231.4	228.1	242.9	276.8	293.4	246.7	257.9	277.5	255.6
Dominica	20.3	23.4	25.8	29.4	32.4	34.1	36.6	39.5	38.2
Grenada	49.6	54.5	55.8	63.7	77.6	76.2	78.6	81.1	85.8
Montserrat	11.2	11.9	13.7	18.1	20.1	17.4	8.4	4.4	4.8
St. Kitts and Nevis	43.6	55.8	67.4	69.8	76.9	63.0	66.8	72.4	75.7
St. Lucia	121.0	144.1	165.6	177.6	207.1	229.5	236.6	253.3	277.6
St. Vincent and the Grenadines	29.4	28.9	41.1	44.0	44.0	52.9	64.0	70.7	74.0
Other Caribbean countries	8,299.4	8,482.9	9,203.2	10,215.2	10,955.2	11,820.7	12,674.5	13,432.5	14,184.9
Bahamas	1,332.9	1,192.7	1,243.5	1,304.0	1,332.6	1,346.2	1,450.0	1,415.9	1,402.8
Cuba	243.4	387.4	567.0	729.0	850.0	1,100.0	1,380.0	1,353.0	1,626.2
Dominican Republic	899.5	877.5	1,054.8	1,070.3	1,147.5	1,568.4	1,765.5	2,099.4	2,141.7
Jamaica	740.0	764.0	858.0	942.0	973.0	1,068.5	1,100.0	1,131.0	1,197.0
Puerto Rico	1,367.0	1,435.7	1,567.4	1,659.4	1,782.3	1,842.1	1,930.2	2,125.0	2,155.6
Others[1]	3,716.6	3,825.6	3,912.5	4,510.5	4,869.8	4,895.5	5,048.8	5,308.2	5,661.6
Memorandum item:									
Share of ECCB in total Caribbean (in percent)	6.1	6.5	6.6	6.7	6.9	6.1	5.9	6.0	5.8

Sources: Eastern Caribbean Central Bank, Caribbean Tourism Organization, and IMF staff estimates.
[1] Includes Barbados, Belize, Bermuda, Cayman Islands, Guyana, Trinidad and Tobago, Turks and Caicos Islands, Aruba, Bonaire, Curaçao, Saba, St. Eustatius, St. Maarten, Guadeloupe, Martinique, Haiti, Suriname, and U.S. Virgin Islands.

Public Finances

Table 24. ECCB Area: Selected Public Sector Indicators by Country
(Percent of GDP)

	1990	1991	1992	1993	1994	1995	1996	1997	1998
Saving	3.6	3.8	4.0	4.7	4.0	4.0	4.0	3.3	3.8
Antigua and Barbuda	−3.2	−3.1	−3.1	−2.2	−1.3	−1.9	0.0	−1.4	−0.1
Dominica	4.1	3.4	2.8	0.8	0.2	2.4	3.0	3.0	3.5
Grenada	0.5	3.0	3.3	5.2	4.1	5.2	5.4	3.1	3.7
St. Kitts and Nevis	3.7	1.0	3.8	4.6	2.1	5.1	0.5	1.3	−1.8
St. Lucia	9.1	9.7	9.7	10.5	9.7	7.9	7.2	6.8	7.3
St. Vincent and the Grenadines	8.4	7.9	6.7	8.3	7.6	6.3	7.4	8.4	9.8
Capital expenditure	8.7	9.1	7.0	8.0	8.4	7.2	7.3	9.3	9.6
Antigua and Barbuda	2.9	3.6	0.9	2.4	4.2	4.8	4.6	7.4	6.4
Dominica	19.3	13.8	8.3	5.8	8.8	11.9	11.4	10.5	9.3
Grenada	11.4	10.2	4.1	8.0	10.0	6.7	10.5	10.9	12.4
St. Kitts and Nevis	4.7	5.3	3.7	7.8	4.9	6.8	7.3	14.3	10.1
St. Lucia	7.2	10.8	11.5	13.1	11.1	8.2	6.7	6.4	9.1
St. Vincent and the Grenadines	14.5	14.3	13.0	9.9	12.2	6.0	6.9	11.5	13.8
Overall balance	−2.4	−2.5	−1.1	−0.7	−2.0	−0.6	−0.6	−3.8	−2.8
Antigua and Barbuda	−4.8	−5.3	−3.1	−3.6	−5.1	−6.3	−3.8	−8.0	−4.8
Dominica	−8.5	−5.7	−1.5	−1.5	−3.6	−1.0	1.4	−1.1	−2.6
Grenada	−7.8	−3.0	1.3	2.5	−1.6	1.6	−1.3	−4.9	−5.8
St. Kitts and Nevis	1.8	−0.5	3.6	−0.2	0.6	1.6	−3.7	−9.6	−8.1
St. Lucia	3.0	0.2	−1.2	0.7	0.7	1.8	2.2	1.3	1.0
St. Vincent and the Grenadines	−0.9	−0.8	−3.4	−1.1	−2.8	1.1	1.6	−1.0	1.7
External financing	3.1	3.3	2.6	1.8	1.9	1.3	1.9	4.1	2.3
Antigua and Barbuda	4.4	5.9	4.4	3.4	3.5	4.1	4.4	5.1	3.3
Dominica	4.5	4.0	1.1	−1.4	−1.2	0.5	−0.1	0.2	0.5
Grenada	6.1	1.3	−0.5	−0.5	1.4	−1.3	0.8	0.6	2.3
St. Kitts and Nevis	1.5	1.4	1.8	2.0	2.1	1.9	2.5	16.3	3.1
St. Lucia	0.7	1.9	3.5	2.2	1.2	1.2	1.9	2.7	1.4
St. Vincent and the Grenadines	2.6	3.9	2.4	2.9	3.1	−1.0	−0.4	0.5	3.1
Domestic financing[1]	−0.8	−0.8	−1.5	−1.1	0.1	−0.7	−1.3	−0.3	0.4
Antigua and Barbuda	0.4	−0.6	−1.3	0.2	1.5	2.2	−0.6	2.9	1.4
Dominica	4.0	1.7	0.4	2.9	4.8	0.5	−1.3	0.9	2.1
Grenada	1.7	1.8	−0.9	−2.0	0.2	−0.3	0.5	4.3	3.5
St. Kitts and Nevis	−3.3	−0.8	−5.3	−1.9	−2.6	−3.5	1.2	−6.7	5.0
St. Lucia	−3.7	−2.2	−2.4	−2.8	−1.9	−3.0	−4.1	−3.9	−2.4
St. Vincent and the Grenadines	−1.7	−3.1	1.0	−1.8	−0.3	−0.1	−1.2	0.5	−4.7

Sources: National authorities, and IMF staff estimates.
[1]Includes privatization proceeds.

ment to over 9 percent of GDP, public saving covered slightly less than 40 percent of investment. The investment of public enterprises has been largely aimed at improving water and sewerage infrastructure, and has been partly financed with loans on favorable terms from the CDB. Net external financing of public enterprise operations averaged about 1 percent of GDP in the period 1990–98. To help cover related debt service obligations and bring water rates to economic levels, some countries have recently acted to ensure adequate metering and to raise charges by linking them more closely to consumption levels.

There are sharp contrasts in public saving and investment performance in the region. Large interest obligations in Antigua and Barbuda (at about 7½ percent of GDP) contributed to negative public saving of close to 2 percent of GDP a year in 1990–98. As a result, Antigua and Barbuda has persistently recorded the lowest public investment in the region (only about 4 percent of GDP on average). The substantial decline in saving in Grenada in 1997–98 coincided with marked increases in public investment financed through domestic commercial borrowing and privatization proceeds. The same combination of low public saving and high public investment in

IV RECENT ECONOMIC DEVELOPMENTS

Table 25. ECCB Area: Public Sector Operations[1]
(Percent of GDP)

	1990	1991	1992	1993	1994	1995	1996	1997	1998
Revenue and grants	31.9	31.8	31.2	32.8	32.6	33.0	33.8	33.4	34.3
Current revenue	29.2	28.9	29.3	30.2	30.2	30.5	31.1	31.3	31.3
Capital revenue	0.6	0.6	0.5	0.5	0.6	0.8	0.7	0.7	0.9
External grants	2.1	2.3	1.3	2.1	1.8	1.7	2.0	1.5	2.2
Expenditure	34.3	34.3	32.3	33.5	34.6	33.6	34.4	37.2	37.1
Current	25.6	25.1	25.3	25.6	26.2	26.4	27.1	27.9	27.5
Of which:									
Wages and salaries	12.5	12.3	12.3	12.6	12.7	13.3	13.4	13.4	13.5
Interest	3.7	3.3	3.3	3.3	3.2	3.2	3.3	3.4	2.9
Capital	8.7	9.1	7.0	8.0	8.4	7.2	7.3	9.3	9.6
Saving	3.6	3.8	4.0	4.7	4.0	4.0	4.0	3.3	3.8
Overall balance	−2.4	−2.5	−1.1	−0.7	−2.0	−0.6	−0.6	−3.8	−2.8
Financing	2.4	2.5	1.1	0.7	2.0	0.6	0.6	3.8	2.8
External	3.1	3.3	2.6	1.8	1.9	1.3	1.9	4.1	2.3
Domestic[2]	−0.8	−0.8	−1.5	−1.1	0.1	−0.7	−1.3	−0.3	0.4

Sources: National authorities, and IMF staff estimates.
[1] The Area excludes Anguilla and Montserrat.
[2] Includes privatization proceeds.

St. Kitts and Nevis resulted in part from the effects of Hurricane Georges in 1998. St. Lucia has funded a comparatively larger share of its public investment effort with public saving in recent years.

For most countries in the region, recent declines in saving have aggravated a key fiscal problem—the lack of sufficient resources to fund public sector investment programs (PSIPs). While investment plans are large and expanding throughout the region, external grant receipts have not grown as fast. Some countries are resorting to other sources to fund selected investment projects. In Grenada, for example, the government entered into lease-to-own arrangements with the private sector for the construction of a stadium and a ministerial complex (Box 6). St. Lucia entered into a similar arrangement for a ministerial building. In Antigua and Barbuda concessions to build, own, operate, and transfer have been arranged for a thermal power plant and a government office complex. These arrangements have involved costly commercial borrowing that is likely to raise the average interest rate on external debt in the years ahead.

Against this background, the financing of the overall public sector deficits has continued to come largely from external sources. External financing averaged 2½ percent of GDP a year in 1990–98 (see Table 25), and about 65 percent of this financing was secured on concessional terms, with the average annual interest rate estimated at 3⅓ percent, and the CDB remaining the main creditor. Domestic financing has been negative in most countries, mainly because the substantial accumulation of financial assets by the social security agencies has continued to exceed increases in net domestic debt by the rest of the public sector. Only about half the financing of central government deficits has been provided by external creditors, with the remainder coming largely from the social security agencies and the domestic banking system.

Low or declining saving has led to comparatively greater reliance on domestic financing for the governments of Antigua and Barbuda, Dominica, and Grenada. For these governments domestic financing averaged over 2½ percent of GDP in 1990–98, with privatization proceeds also being of key importance for Grenada in recent years. The stock of net domestic bank credit to governments in the region has remained at 6½–8 percent of GDP recently (Table 31).

The region's gross public debt in relation to GDP is estimated to have remained broadly unchanged. By end-1998 gross public debt stood at 63 percent of GDP (Table 32), with external debt at some 45 percent of GDP, about half of it denominated in U.S. dollars. There are sharp differences in the external debt burden across the region, with Antigua and Barbuda accounting for a little over one third of the regional external debt. Recently concluded bilateral rescheduling agreements will help reduce Antigua and Barbuda's debt service, while substantial borrowing to fund investment projects has resulted in marked increases in the external debt to GDP ratio of

Money and Banking

Table 26. ECCB Area: Selected Central Government Indicators by Country
(Percent of GDP)

	1990	1991	1992	1993	1994	1995	1996	1997	1998
Saving	1.8	2.0	2.0	2.6	1.7	2.1	1.9	0.9	0.6
Antigua and Barbuda	−1.1	−1.0	−0.8	−1.4	−1.7	−1.1	0.0	−2.1	−2.7
Dominica	1.9	1.2	1.3	−0.6	−0.8	0.9	1.2	0.9	0.9
Grenada	−3.0	−0.5	−0.5	1.7	0.1	2.2	2.1	−0.3	0.2
St. Kitts and Nevis	2.1	−0.3	0.4	2.5	0.7	2.9	0.2	0.4	−2.3
St. Lucia	5.4	5.9	6.3	7.1	6.3	4.3	3.6	3.2	3.6
St. Vincent and the Grenadines	5.0	4.6	2.8	4.1	4.0	3.3	3.8	4.0	4.2
Capital expenditure	6.2	6.6	5.3	6.1	6.5	5.9	5.9	6.5	7.0
Antigua and Barbuda	1.8	3.0	0.9	2.1	4.2	3.7	2.5	3.0	2.5
Dominica	14.6	10.3	7.8	5.3	8.2	10.3	9.6	9.4	8.3
Grenada	9.6	8.9	3.0	4.7	6.7	5.8	9.7	8.7	9.9
St. Kitts and Nevis	3.5	3.9	3.2	4.3	3.8	6.5	4.9	6.1	6.9
St. Lucia	5.2	5.8	7.3	11.1	9.0	7.0	6.5	5.8	8.0
St. Vincent and the Grenadines	8.4	11.2	10.7	7.3	6.6	3.5	4.7	10.3	10.0
Overall balance	−2.2	−2.4	−1.8	−1.7	−2.9	−1.9	−1.8	−3.8	−4.0
Antigua and Barbuda	−1.8	−3.3	−0.8	−2.8	−5.4	−4.4	−1.7	−4.3	−3.8
Dominica	−6.8	−4.6	−2.7	−2.6	−4.9	−3.0	−0.6	−2.8	−4.3
Grenada	−9.8	−5.4	−1.8	−0.2	−3.5	−0.6	−3.7	−6.2	−6.8
St. Kitts and Nevis	−0.2	−2.8	−1.7	−1.1	−2.0	−2.4	−3.9	−4.6	−7.8
St. Lucia	1.0	0.6	−0.9	−0.8	−0.7	−0.9	−1.3	−1.8	−1.6
St. Vincent and the Grenadines	1.3	−1.6	−5.2	−2.8	−1.0	0.5	0.2	−4.5	−2.6
External financing	2.1	1.8	1.0	0.6	0.7	0.4	1.1	2.0	1.7
Antigua and Barbuda	−0.1	1.4	−0.3	−0.5	0.1	0.4	1.8	0.2	0.1
Dominica	4.9	4.1	1.2	−1.2	−0.4	0.1	−0.7	0.0	0.6
Grenada	6.1	1.3	−0.2	−0.4	1.1	−1.5	0.8	0.5	2.7
St. Kitts and Nevis	1.5	1.4	1.8	1.0	1.8	1.7	1.2	8.6	3.4
St. Lucia	1.0	0.7	2.0	1.6	1.0	1.5	2.3	2.9	1.5
St. Vincent and the Grenadines	2.5	3.9	2.0	2.6	1.2	−1.1	−1.3	1.0	3.3
Domestic financing[1]	0.1	0.6	0.8	1.1	2.2	1.6	0.7	1.8	2.3
Antigua and Barbuda	1.9	1.9	1.0	3.3	5.3	4.0	−0.1	4.1	3.7
Dominica	1.9	0.5	1.5	3.8	5.3	3.0	1.3	2.8	3.6
Grenada	3.7	4.1	2.1	0.6	2.4	2.0	2.9	5.7	4.0
St. Kitts and Nevis	−1.2	1.4	−0.1	0.1	0.3	0.7	2.7	−4.0	4.4
St. Lucia	−2.0	−1.3	−1.1	−0.8	−0.3	−0.6	−1.0	−1.1	0.1
St. Vincent and the Grenadines	−3.8	−2.2	3.2	0.1	−0.1	0.6	1.1	3.4	−0.8

Sources: National authorities; and IMF staff estimates.
[1]Includes privatization proceeds.

St. Kitts and Nevis, and to a lesser extent, of St. Lucia. Debt forgiveness extended by the British government to Dominica and Grenada helped reduce the regional stocks of external debt in 1997.[34]

External arrears have been a major problem for only a few of the countries. Antigua and Barbuda, which accounted for nearly 95 percent of the regional total in 1998 (Table 33), managed to reduce external arrears to bilateral creditors through rescheduling agreements, but the total stock outstanding remained quite high and was mostly due to private creditors.

Money and Banking

The stock of broad money doubled during the period 1990–98, from a little more than half a percent of GDP to almost three-fourth's (see Table 3). This increase, together with sizable foreign borrowing by commercial banks, helped finance an equally strong rise in outstanding bank credit to the private sector. The fastest growth in credit to the private sector was recorded in Grenada (153 percent) and the slowest in Dominica (94 percent) and in Anguilla and Montserrat (40 percent) (Table 34). During 1999, the stocks of both broad money and credit to the private sector

[34]Debt forgiveness was also extended to Montserrat.

IV RECENT ECONOMIC DEVELOPMENTS

Table 27. ECCB Area: Central Government Operations[1]
(Percent of GDP)

	1990	1991	1992	1993	1994	1995	1996	1997	1998
Revenue and grants	26.3	25.8	25.2	26.5	26.2	26.8	27.4	26.8	27.2
Current	24.1	23.7	23.8	24.6	24.4	24.9	25.2	25.1	24.8
Tax revenue	21.5	21.1	20.9	21.4	21.1	21.4	21.5	21.4	21.3
International trade	7.1	6.4	6.2	6.3	6.1	6.0	6.2	6.3	6.1
Income	4.4	4.5	5.0	4.9	4.9	5.1	4.9	4.7	4.8
Personal	1.2	1.1	1.2	1.3	1.3	1.9	1.7	1.6	1.6
Corporate	2.8	2.9	3.4	3.1	3.1	2.7	2.6	2.5	2.5
Goods and services	9.3	9.3	9.2	9.6	9.6	9.8	9.7	9.8	9.9
Other	0.7	1.0	0.5	0.6	0.5	0.6	0.6	0.6	0.5
Nontax revenue	2.5	2.5	2.9	3.2	3.3	3.5	3.8	3.7	3.5
Capital revenue	0.3	0.3	0.2	0.2	0.2	0.2	0.2	0.3	0.6
External grants	1.9	1.9	1.1	1.7	1.6	1.7	2.0	1.5	1.8
Expenditure	28.5	28.3	27.0	28.2	29.1	28.7	29.2	30.7	31.2
Current	22.2	21.7	21.8	22.0	22.6	22.8	23.4	24.1	24.1
Wages and salaries	12.0	11.8	11.7	12.0	12.1	12.5	12.5	12.5	12.6
Goods and services	4.8	4.6	4.8	4.5	4.8	4.8	5.1	5.4	5.4
Interest	2.4	2.0	1.9	2.0	2.0	2.0	2.2	2.5	2.4
Domestic	1.5	1.3	1.2	1.3	1.3	1.3	1.4	1.4	1.4
External	0.8	0.7	0.7	0.7	0.7	0.7	0.8	1.0	1.0
Transfers	3.1	3.3	3.3	3.4	3.7	3.6	3.5	3.7	3.8
To rest of public sector	0.5	0.5	0.6	0.6	0.6	0.6	0.5	0.6	0.6
Abroad	0.5	0.7	0.5	0.6	0.6	0.7	0.7	0.6	0.7
Pensions	1.3	1.3	1.4	1.3	1.4	1.4	1.4	1.5	1.5
Other to domestic private sector	0.5	0.6	0.5	0.6	0.8	0.7	0.7	0.7	0.7
Capital	6.2	6.6	5.3	6.1	6.5	5.9	5.9	6.5	7.0
Saving	1.8	2.0	2.0	2.6	1.7	2.1	1.9	0.9	0.6
Overall balance	−2.2	−2.4	−1.8	−1.7	−2.9	−1.9	−1.8	−3.8	−4.0
Financing	2.2	2.4	1.8	1.7	2.9	1.9	1.8	3.8	4.0
External	2.1	1.8	1.0	0.6	0.7	0.4	1.1	2.0	1.7
Domestic[2]	0.1	0.6	0.8	1.1	2.2	1.6	0.7	1.8	2.3

Sources: National authorities, and IMF staff estimates.
[1]The Area excludes Anguilla and Montserrat.
[2]Includes privatization proceeds.

grew by around 10 percent, similar to the rates recorded during 1997 and 1998. At the regional level, the expansion in private sector credit was concentrated in service industries including entertainment and catering and professional and other services, as well as personal loans to individuals, mainly for the acquisition of property (Table 35). The rise in bank mortgage lending was reflected in the maturity structure of banks' loan portfolios, as the share of loans with a maturity of five years or more rose sharply, to almost 50 percent at end-1998 (Table 36).

The stock of net bank credit to the public sector declined over this period, as the increase in net credit to governments was more than offset by deposits from the region's social security schemes (see Table 31). However, during 1999, these deposits declined slightly, while net bank credit to governments increased sharply (by over 12 percent). the stock of net credit from the ECCB to member governments actually fell during 1990–98, as both gross ECCB credit to governments declined and governments' deposits at the ECCB rose, notably in 1998.

The region's official net international reserves rose by almost US$160 million during the period, to over US$350 million at end-1998 (see Table 3), and were roughly unchanged during 1999. The foreign exchange backing ratio was maintained at an average of about 95 percent (see Table 4). At the same time, commercial banks reduced their net foreign assets somewhat, to help finance domestic credit expansion. The banks' net external borrowing was particularly heavy in 1996 and 1997 when credit expanded rapidly in most countries. New borrowing was negligible in 1998, but was heavy once again in 1999; in both years the banks added substantially to their gross foreign assets. The rise

Money and Banking

Table 28. ECCB Area: Central Government Expenditure Indicators by Country
(Percent of GDP)

	1990	1991	1992	1993	1994	1995	1996	1997	1998
Current expenditure	22.2	21.7	21.8	22.0	22.6	22.8	23.4	24.1	24.1
Antigua and Barbuda	22.2	21.0	22.0	21.7	22.3	22.7	21.8	22.8	22.9
Dominica	26.2	26.9	26.4	27.5	26.5	25.5	26.6	28.2	28.0
Grenada	26.9	24.5	23.9	24.0	23.9	23.0	23.0	24.4	25.1
St. Kitts and Nevis	21.9	22.1	23.1	23.1	26.1	27.1	30.0	29.6	31.7
St. Lucia	18.1	18.1	17.6	18.5	18.8	19.8	20.4	21.0	20.1
St. Vincent and the Grenadines	22.8	22.8	22.9	22.4	23.6	23.3	24.1	24.2	23.5
Wage bill	12.0	11.8	11.7	12.0	12.1	12.5	12.5	12.5	12.6
Antigua and Barbuda	11.7	11.8	12.3	12.0	11.9	12.5	12.0	11.4	12.4
Dominica	15.3	15.6	14.7	15.4	15.2	14.6	14.8	15.2	14.9
Grenada	13.8	12.8	13.1	12.9	12.0	12.0	12.3	13.0	12.4
St. Kitts and Nevis	11.6	11.2	11.2	12.0	12.7	14.0	14.8	13.9	14.9
St. Lucia	9.7	9.3	9.1	9.7	10.1	11.1	11.0	11.1	10.7
St. Vincent and the Grenadines	12.7	12.9	12.7	13.1	13.3	13.1	13.1	13.6	13.0
Spending on goods and services	4.8	4.6	4.8	4.5	4.8	4.8	5.1	5.4	5.4
Antigua and Barbuda	5.1	5.3	5.1	4.9	5.1	5.0	4.6	5.3	5.1
Dominica	5.2	5.2	5.2	5.2	5.0	5.0	5.1	5.6	5.7
Grenada	6.1	4.0	3.9	3.5	4.3	3.9	4.1	3.8	4.3
St. Kitts and Nevis	4.0	4.5	6.0	5.7	6.7	6.8	9.3	10.0	10.8
St. Lucia	3.7	4.1	3.9	3.9	3.9	3.9	4.0	4.2	3.7
St. Vincent and the Grenadines	5.6	5.0	6.0	4.7	5.2	5.1	5.5	5.3	5.1
Interest	2.4	2.0	1.9	2.0	2.0	2.0	2.2	2.5	2.4
Antigua and Barbuda	4.3	2.9	3.1	3.2	3.2	3.1	3.2	4.3	3.1
Dominica	1.6	2.0	2.2	2.3	2.3	2.4	2.7	2.8	2.6
Grenada	3.4	3.1	2.6	2.6	2.4	2.0	2.2	2.3	2.6
St. Kitts and Nevis	2.9	2.8	2.7	2.5	2.6	2.3	3.0	2.8	3.1
St. Lucia	0.8	0.7	0.7	0.8	0.7	0.8	0.9	1.0	1.4
St. Vincent and the Grenadines	0.7	1.1	1.0	1.2	1.3	1.7	1.7	1.6	1.9
Current transfers	3.1	3.3	3.3	3.4	3.7	3.6	3.5	3.7	3.8
Antigua and Barbuda	1.1	1.1	1.5	1.5	2.1	2.1	2.1	1.9	2.3
Dominica	4.0	4.1	4.3	4.7	4.1	3.4	4.0	4.6	4.8
Grenada	3.5	4.6	4.3	5.0	5.3	5.1	4.4	5.3	5.8
St. Kitts and Nevis	3.3	3.5	3.2	2.9	4.1	4.0	2.9	2.9	2.9
St. Lucia	3.9	4.0	3.9	4.0	4.1	4.0	4.5	4.7	4.3
St. Vincent and the Grenadines	3.8	3.8	3.2	3.4	3.8	3.5	3.8	3.8	3.6

Sources: National authorities, and IMF staff estimates.

in the commercial banks' liquidity needs was also reflected in a marked decline in bankers' fixed deposits at the ECCB (see Table 4). These deposits are callable in U.S. dollars and carry an interest rate linked to LIBOR.

Currency held by the public as a share of bank liabilities to the private sector fell from 10 percent at end-1990 to 7 percent at end-1998 (Table 37), reflecting a decline in currency demand associated with technical change in the banking industry. The composition of quasi-money also changed, with a rising share of savings and foreign currency deposits and a falling share of time deposits. The decline in the demand for time deposits is attributable to an anomaly in the yield curve, as interest rates on many short-term time deposits were reportedly below the statutory minimum of 4 percentage points set on passbook savings. As most foreign currency deposits are held by businesses, the rise in the share of foreign currency deposits may be related to attempts by a growing number of companies to economize on foreign exchange transaction costs.[35] The proportion of foreign currency deposits held by nonresidents increased from 17 percent at end-1990 to over 23 percent at end-1998.

---

[35]A levy of 1 percent on the purchase of foreign exchange remains in effect in Antigua and Barbuda. Foreign exchange levies of differing levels also exist in Anguilla and Montserrat.

IV RECENT ECONOMIC DEVELOPMENTS

Table 29. ECCB Area: Central Government Revenue Indicators by Country
(Percent of GDP)

	1990	1991	1992	1993	1994	1995	1996	1997	1998
Tax revenue	21.5	21.1	20.9	21.4	21.1	21.4	21.5	21.4	21.3
Antigua and Barbuda	18.4	17.4	17.6	17.1	17.5	18.5	18.5	18.1	17.5
Dominica	25.6	24.9	24.3	23.4	22.1	22.9	23.3	23.6	23.8
Grenada	22.1	21.7	21.4	23.0	21.7	22.6	22.8	22.0	22.8
St. Kitts and Nevis	19.6	19.3	19.7	21.4	21.2	21.5	21.6	22.1	21.9
St. Lucia	21.9	22.2	22.0	22.9	22.5	21.9	21.4	21.7	21.2
St. Vincent and the Grenadines	24.7	23.7	22.3	22.8	23.8	23.3	24.3	24.3	24.5
Income tax revenue	4.4	4.5	5.0	4.9	4.9	5.1	4.9	4.7	4.8
Antigua and Barbuda	2.6	2.1	2.1	1.9	1.9	2.1	1.6	1.8	1.7
Dominica	7.2	7.0	6.2	5.8	6.4	6.9	6.8	6.7	6.7
Grenada	0.0	0.8	5.0	5.4	4.9	5.8	4.2	2.6	3.1
St. Kitts and Nevis	4.7	4.2	4.1	4.1	4.6	4.8	4.9	5.2	5.7
St. Lucia	6.0	6.3	6.3	6.2	6.4	6.2	6.2	6.4	6.0
St. Vincent and the Grenadines	7.1	7.4	6.8	6.6	7.8	6.7	7.4	7.5	7.9
Taxes on goods and services[1]	9.3	9.3	9.2	9.6	9.6	9.8	9.7	9.8	9.9
Antigua and Barbuda	7.4	7.6	8.0	7.7	7.8	8.4	8.5	8.0	7.9
Dominica	13.2	12.2	11.8	12.2	11.8	12.0	11.9	12.1	12.6
Grenada	12.1	11.1	10.4	11.7	11.7	11.6	12.1	12.9	13.1
St. Kitts and Nevis	7.2	7.6	8.0	8.8	8.5	8.9	9.5	9.5	9.4
St. Lucia	8.4	8.7	8.7	9.2	9.0	8.9	8.3	8.4	8.6
St. Vincent and the Grenadines	10.3	10.2	9.7	10.3	10.8	11.1	10.9	11.1	11.2
International trade taxes[2]	7.1	6.4	6.2	6.3	6.1	6.0	6.2	6.3	6.1
Antigua and Barbuda	8.1	7.4	7.3	7.3	7.6	7.7	8.0	8.0	7.7
Dominica	5.4	5.2	5.1	4.6	4.1	4.1	4.1	4.3	4.2
Grenada	7.7	5.9	5.4	5.2	4.6	4.6	5.8	6.0	6.1
St. Kitts and Nevis	7.3	7.0	7.1	8.0	7.6	7.3	6.8	6.9	6.4
St. Lucia	6.9	6.5	6.5	6.8	6.6	6.3	6.4	6.4	6.1
St. Vincent and the Grenadines	6.4	5.3	4.7	4.6	4.0	4.1	4.3	4.3	4.0
Nontax revenue	2.5	2.5	2.9	3.2	3.3	3.5	3.8	3.7	3.5
Antigua and Barbuda	2.8	2.6	3.6	3.2	3.1	3.1	3.3	2.7	2.7
Dominica	2.4	3.2	3.4	3.5	3.6	3.4	4.5	5.5	5.1
Grenada	1.8	2.3	2.1	2.6	2.3	2.6	2.3	2.1	2.5
St. Kitts and Nevis	4.4	2.5	3.8	4.2	5.6	8.5	8.6	8.0	7.5
St. Lucia	1.7	1.8	1.9	2.7	2.5	2.2	2.6	2.6	2.5
St. Vincent and the Grenadines	3.1	3.7	3.5	3.8	3.7	3.4	3.7	3.9	3.2
External grants	1.9	1.9	1.1	1.7	1.6	1.7	2.0	1.5	1.8
Antigua and Barbuda	0.5	0.3	0.7	0.5	0.2	0.0	0.4	0.5	0.9
Dominica	5.4	3.9	2.8	2.5	3.7	6.0	7.6	5.3	2.6
Grenada	2.6	3.6	1.7	2.7	3.1	2.6	3.8	2.7	2.8
St. Kitts and Nevis	0.8	1.1	0.6	0.3	1.0	1.1	0.3	0.2	0.6
St. Lucia	0.5	0.4	0.1	3.1	2.0	1.7	1.4	0.7	2.4
St. Vincent and the Grenadines	4.6	5.0	2.7	0.3	1.0	0.4	1.0	1.6	1.6

Sources: National authorities, and IMF staff estimates.
[1] Includes consumption tax on imports.
[2] Includes import duties, customs charges, foreign exchange tax, guest and hotel taxes, and cruise passenger tax.

There is considerable variation in deposit and lending interest rates across countries, reflecting the influence of market imperfections that have hindered arbitrage (see Table 7). In 1998, for instance, the average spread between lending and deposit rates ranged from a high of 8 percentage points in Grenada, to a low of 6.4 percentage points in St. Kitts and Nevis. The scarcity of investment alternatives during this stage of development of the financial system contributed to low deposit rates. On the other hand, regulatory distortions, the high unit cost of the banks, imperfect competition in the industry, and capital account restrictions hindered the equalization of factor returns and led to relatively high lending rates.

Table 30. ECCB Area: Average Import Duties and Customs Surcharges

	1990	1991	1992	1993	1994	1995	1996	1997	1998
	(Percent)								
Import duty[1]	8.4	7.5	7.5	7.1	7.0	7.0	7.2	7.4	7.2
Antigua and Barbuda	6.9	6.1	5.8	5.8	5.8	5.6	6.3	6.5	6.1
Dominica	7.3	8.3	8.9	8.4	7.5	7.1	7.7	8.0	8.7
Grenada	12.7	9.2	9.2	6.8	7.0	6.7	6.4	6.6	5.9
St. Kitts and Nevis	...	...	...	...	...	...	...	10.0	9.6
St. Lucia	8.8	8.1	8.3	8.7	8.4	8.5	9.0	8.4	8.6
St. Vincent and the Grenadines	7.4	7.3	7.1	6.4	6.0	6.9	6.2	5.4	5.2
Import duty and surcharges[2]	9.4	8.7	8.8	9.1	9.3	9.5	10.3	10.4	10.2
Antigua and Barbuda	8.4	7.5	7.2	7.2	8.0	8.1	8.8	9.1	8.8
Dominica	8.3	9.3	9.9	9.4	8.6	8.2	9.0	9.2	10.0
Grenada	12.7	9.2	9.2	8.8	9.3	9.1	11.0	11.3	10.2
St. Kitts and Nevis	...	...	...	...	...	...	...	11.3	10.2
St. Lucia	10.5	10.0	10.6	11.5	11.7	12.2	13.0	12.2	12.4
St. Vincent and the Grenadines	7.4	7.3	7.1	8.3	8.0	8.7	8.7	7.6	7.3
	(Percent of GDP)								
Import duty	4.8	4.3	4.0	3.8	3.6	3.5	3.6	3.7	3.7
Antigua and Barbuda	4.1	3.8	3.7	3.6	3.5	3.4	3.8	3.6	3.4
Dominica	4.6	4.4	4.3	3.8	3.3	3.3	3.3	3.4	3.4
Grenada	6.1	4.3	3.8	3.2	3.2	3.1	3.2	3.2	3.2
St. Kitts and Nevis	...	...	...	...	...	...	...	4.7	4.6
St. Lucia	5.1	4.7	4.5	4.6	4.3	4.1	4.2	4.2	4.0
St. Vincent and the Grenadines	4.5	4.1	3.6	3.2	2.9	3.1	2.8	2.8	2.8
Import duty and surcharges[2]	5.4	4.9	4.7	4.8	4.8	4.9	5.2	5.3	5.2
Antigua and Barbuda	5.1	4.7	4.6	4.5	4.8	4.9	5.2	5.1	4.9
Dominica	5.2	5.0	4.8	4.3	3.8	3.8	3.8	3.9	3.8
Grenada	6.1	4.3	3.8	4.2	4.2	4.3	5.5	5.5	5.6
St. Kitts and Nevis	...	...	...	...	...	...	...	6.0	5.8
St. Lucia	6.0	5.8	5.8	6.1	6.0	6.0	6.1	6.2	5.8
St. Vincent and the Grenadines	4.5	4.1	3.6	4.1	3.8	4.0	4.0	4.0	3.9

Sources: Eastern Caribbean Central Bank, and IMF staff estimates.
[1]Import duty collections as percent of merchandise imports.
[2]Revenue from import duty and custom charges as percent of merchandise imports.

Interest rate spreads are wide in the ECCB area. The production cost elasticity of deposits in the area has been estimated at 1.35 for the period 1991–96, suggesting the presence of short-run scale diseconomies in commercial banking.[36] A little more than one half of the interest rate spread during this period was attributable to operational costs and provisions for loan losses. Reserve requirements accounted for an additional 6 percent of the interest rate spread, and the remaining 41 percent of the spread was estimated as the implicit equity return (equivalent to nearly 3 percentage points). The 4 percent statutory minimum deposit rate was estimated to add significantly to the cost of bank intermediation, which also reflected high fixed costs, including those stemming from capital controls (largely invariant over the period), and high operating costs.

External Sector

With the fixed exchange rate and the openness of the island economies, movements in the real effective value of the Eastern Caribbean dollar closely mirror the behavior of the U.S. dollar vis-a-vis other major currencies. Differential trading patterns and relative price behavior in the countries in the region play an important role in the evolution of the real effective exchange rates calculated for the individual countries (Table 38 and Figure 1). During 1990–98, the Eastern Caribbean dollar appreciated in real effective terms in all countries by about 11

---
[36]Ruby Randall, *Interest Rate Spreads in the Eastern Caribbean*, IMF Working Paper (WP/98/59, April 1998).

Box 6. Government Lease-to-Own Liabilities: The Case of Grenada

In 1997 the government signed two lease-to-own contracts with private investors for the construction of a ministerial complex and a stadium to be financed by domestic banks and a foreign bank. Under these arrangements, the two facilities were to be built over a period of two to three years and subsequently leased to the government for a period of 15 years. Although legal ownership of the facilities is to be transferred to the government only at the end of the lease period, an effective transfer of ownership will take place when the facilities are completed and made available to the government. At that time, all the risks and rewards of ownership will be transferred from the legal owners to the user of the facilities. The investors have set up resident corporations to arrange the construction of these facilities, their financing, and leasing to the government.

- In the case of the stadium, the total construction cost is estimated at US$28.6 million. Financing is being provided by the CLICO Investment Bank of Trinidad and Tobago, with an initial disbursement (US$4.6 million) made at the time of the signing of the agreement (May 9, 1997), and the balance (US$18.4 million) disbursed on a quarterly basis over the estimated construction period (1998–2000). The capital cost will be repaid by means of interim bonds and permanent 15-year maturity bonds (for the balance of the principal) issued in favor of the foreign bank by the private resident company, the National Stadium Project Corporation (NSPC). Interest would be at a rate of 11 percent per annum on the interim bonds of the initial advance, and at a floating market rate for the permanent bonds, and would be paid (together with the amortization amounts) in semiannual installments. Rent paid by the government (charged against the Budget's Consolidated Fund) to the NSPC would be used to pay off the amortization and interest owed to the foreign bank, which would receive rental payments directly in case of a default by the NSPC. Imports of equipment and machinery for the project were exempted from all taxes, and remittances due to the foreign bank are free of withholding tax.

- Construction of the ministerial complex was completed in 18 months (March 1999) at a cost of US$13 million. Financing was provided by three domestic banks and the National Insurance Scheme through loans made to the private company created to manage the operation. After completion, the complex was transferred to the government under an arrangement that requires semiannual lease payments over a 15-year period at an implicit interest rate of 11 percent.

The government did not incur any cash payments before the completion of the two facilities, but will make substantial rental payments, amounting to US$2.1 million in 2000, and about US$5.9 million annually in subsequent years. In the government accounts, these payments could be divided into interest charges and debt repayments, with the latter reducing the value of the claim of the lessor on the lessee. In the year 2002, for example, projected rental payments will raise government debt service by 1.4 percent of GDP.

---

percent, except for Dominica (7½ percent) and Grenada (over 5 percent).[37] In 1999, there was a further real appreciation of some 5 percent in St. Lucia and about 2 percent in both Antigua and Barbuda and St. Kitts and Nevis, but virtually no change in the other countries.

Trade has been liberalized with the implementation of the Common External Tariff (CET) under the CARICOM Agreement of 1992, which committed the signatories to reduce import tariffs to a maximum of 20 percent over six years starting in 1993.[38] All countries in the region reduced the maximum tariff to 35 percent in 1993, but since then progress in this area has proceeded at differing paces, with St. Vincent and the Grenadines adhering strictly to the timetable for phased reductions and Antigua and Barbuda and St. Kitts and Nevis lagging the most (Table 39). The slow progress has been related mostly to concerns about the effect of tariff reductions on government revenue and on certain domestic activities.

While the scheduled tariff reductions are considerable, their impact on tax collections and on the level of protection is lessened by the prevalence of a broad range of exemptions, which are set out in four lists. List A allows protection at the national level for goods that are not considered import-competing (that is, when production in the region does not account for 75 percent of regional demand). List B exempts certain goods that are sensitive to the cost of living in the OECS territories and Belize. List C includes goods to which minimum rates apply, including alcoholic beverages, tobacco products, petro-

---

[37]As measured by the real effective exchange rate indexes, calculated by the IMF, which use relative consumer prices. Lack of data precludes the calculation of indexes based on unit labor costs or wages.

[38]The CET is a tariff schedule with several rates. The 20 percent maximum tariff applies to noncompeting final goods and agroindustry products. A higher duty rate applies to agriculture (40 percent), and lower rates to agricultural inputs (zero), noncompeting primary inputs (5 percent), and competing inputs (10 percent or 15 percent) (Table 40).

Table 31. ECCB Area: Banking System Credit to the Public Sector

	1990	1991	1992	1993	1994	1995	1996	1997	1998
	(Millions of Eastern Caribbean dollars)								
Public sector (net)[1]	97.0	62.4	12.6	33.6	−6.2	29.1	32.5	21.4	−46.7
Gross credit[2]	571.7	573.4	607.9	659.4	704.9	854.4	921.2	967.8	1,121.9
Deposits[3]	474.7	511.0	595.3	625.8	711.0	825.3	888.7	946.4	1,168.7
Central government (net)	372.7	359.7	307.1	341.0	336.6	401.2	449.5	464.2	454.3
Gross credit[2]	458.0	463.0	467.0	493.4	497.2	599.8	651.7	688.2	818.7
Deposits[3]	85.3	103.3	159.9	152.4	160.6	198.6	202.2	224.0	364.4
	(Percent of GDP)								
Public sector (net)[1]	2.5	1.5	0.3	0.7	−0.1	0.5	0.6	0.4	−0.7
Gross credit[2]	14.7	13.7	13.6	13.7	14.2	16.1	16.7	16.5	18.2
Deposits[3]	12.2	12.2	13.3	13.0	14.3	15.6	16.1	16.2	16.8
Central government (net)	9.6	8.6	6.9	7.1	6.8	7.6	8.2	7.9	6.5
Gross credit[2]	11.8	11.0	10.4	10.3	10.0	11.3	11.8	11.8	11.8
Deposits[3]	2.2	2.5	3.6	3.2	3.2	3.7	3.7	3.8	5.9

Sources: Eastern Caribbean Central Bank, and IMF staff estimates.
[1]Includes the central government; nonfinancial public enterprises; and social security systems.
[2]Includes loans and advances, treasury bills, debentures, and other securities.
[3]Includes fixed deposits, call accounts, and sinking funds.

Table 32. ECCB Area: Public Sector Debt
(Percent of GDP; end of period)

	1990	1991	1992	1993	1994	1995	1996	1997	1998
Total debt	57.3	63.5	62.8	62.1	63.5	66.6	64.6	62.2	63.3
Antigua and Barbuda	91.3	122.2	125.8	121.4	119.8	132.3	120.0	108.5	108.3
Dominica	68.5	71.5	67.5	65.8	67.4	68.2	62.6	55.8	53.8
Grenada	63.2	53.3	47.1	45.5	46.5	44.9	45.8	45.1	43.0
St. Kitts and Nevis	54.1	54.2	50.2	45.3	45.5	54.4	62.6	70.2	76.1
St. Lucia	25.2	24.1	28.3	29.0	29.4	30.8	32.4	33.6	34.1
St. Vincent and the Grenadines	44.2	44.6	44.9	47.2	52.1	50.3	47.4	44.6	49.7
External debt[1]	42.6	49.8	49.2	48.4	49.3	50.5	47.9	45.7	45.1
Antigua and Barbuda	77.5	109.8	113.0	106.7	105.8	115.4	103.2	91.1	88.8
Dominica	51.6	52.3	50.8	47.4	46.1	47.2	44.1	36.7	35.3
Grenada	47.7	37.8	35.0	34.2	35.5	34.4	33.4	30.8	28.3
St. Kitts and Nevis	25.1	25.4	24.3	23.7	23.7	23.6	24.8	37.5	38.7
St. Lucia	17.0	18.2	19.4	20.1	20.4	21.1	22.6	23.9	22.8
St. Vincent and the Grenadines	28.4	31.0	30.4	32.4	36.1	33.7	31.9	29.7	35.5
Domestic debt[2]	14.7	13.7	13.6	13.7	14.2	16.1	16.7	16.5	18.2
Antigua and Barbuda	13.8	12.4	12.8	14.7	14.1	16.9	16.8	17.4	19.6
Dominica	17.0	19.2	16.7	18.5	21.3	21.0	18.5	19.1	18.5
Grenada	15.5	15.5	12.1	11.3	11.0	10.5	12.5	14.3	14.7
St. Kitts and Nevis	29.1	28.9	25.9	21.6	21.9	30.8	37.8	32.7	37.4
St. Lucia	8.2	5.9	8.9	8.9	9.0	9.7	9.8	9.7	11.3
St. Vincent and the Grenadines	15.7	13.6	14.5	14.7	16.1	16.6	15.5	14.8	14.2

Sources: Eastern Caribbean Central Bank, and IMF staff estimates.
[1]Includes external arrears.
[2]Data refer to the financial system's gross credit to the public sector.

IV RECENT ECONOMIC DEVELOPMENTS

Table 33. ECCB Area: External Arrears
(Millions of U.S. dollars)

	1990	1991	1992	1993	1994	1995	1996	1997	1998
By borrower									
Central government	65.1	60.7	71.2	78.2	88.7	90.9	87.2	84.8	91.2
Antigua and Barbuda	41.6	50.0	60.8	67.7	78.0	80.7	77.1	76.2	80.6
Dominica	0.0	0.5	0.6	0.9	1.1	1.9	1.8	0.8	0.4
Grenada	23.1	9.8	9.2	9.2	9.2	7.4	7.7	7.2	8.8
St. Kitts and Nevis	0.0	0.0	0.1	0.2	0.4	0.4	0.5	0.5	0.4
St. Lucia	0.2	0.3	0.3	0.1	0.0	0.1	0.1	0.1	1.0
St. Vincent and the Grenadines	0.1	0.0	0.2	0.1	0.0	0.4	0.0	0.0	0.0
Statutory bodies	114.6	143.2	170.7	186.8	212.8	242.9	244.3	229.8	251.2
Antigua and Barbuda	114.3	142.3	170.6	186.6	212.5	242.3	242.1	227.2	244.1
Dominica	0.0	0.0	0.0	0.1	0.0	0.0	0.1	0.1	0.1
Grenada	0.0	0.0	0.0	0.0	0.0	0.0	1.0	1.9	2.7
St. Kitts and Nevis	0.0	0.0	0.0	0.0	0.0	0.0	0.0	0.3	1.2
St. Lucia	0.3	0.9	0.0	0.0	0.1	0.1	0.1	0.1	3.1
St. Vincent and the Grenadines	0.0	0.0	0.0	0.1	0.1	0.5	1.1	0.2	0.0
By creditor category									
Bilateral	18.8	16.7	17.2	18.1	19.4	19.4	20.8	20.7	12.4
Antigua and Barbuda	9.3	9.2	10.3	11.2	12.2	11.6	12.8	13.7	3.0
Dominica	0.0	0.5	0.6	1.0	1.1	1.7	1.3	0.5	0.4
Grenada	9.3	6.6	5.9	5.9	6.0	6.1	6.7	6.5	7.6
St. Kitts and Nevis	0.0	0.0	0.0	0.0	0.1	0.0	0.0	0.0	0.3
St. Lucia	0.1	0.3	0.3	0.0	0.0	0.0	0.0	0.0	1.1
St. Vincent and the Grenadines	0.0	0.0	0.0	0.0	0.0	0.0	0.0	0.0	0.0
Multilateral	8.8	10.0	10.4	11.2	12.1	8.9	3.8	2.3	5.7
Antigua and Barbuda	6.2	7.4	7.3	8.0	9.0	7.0	2.1	0.4	1.4
Dominica	0.0	0.0	0.0	0.0	0.0	0.3	0.5	0.4	0.1
Grenada	2.4	2.4	2.6	2.7	2.6	0.5	0.5	0.7	1.3
St. Kitts and Nevis	0.0	0.0	0.1	0.2	0.3	0.4	0.4	0.5	0.6
St. Lucia	0.0	0.1	0.1	0.1	0.1	0.2	0.2	0.1	2.3
St. Vincent and the Grenadines	0.1	0.0	0.2	0.2	0.1	0.6	0.0	0.2	0.1
Other	151.9	176.4	214.4	235.7	269.9	305.7	306.9	291.5	324.8
Antigua and Barbuda	140.4	175.6	213.7	235.0	269.3	304.4	304.3	289.3	320.3
Dominica	0.0	0.0	0.0	0.0	0.0	0.0	0.0	0.0	0.0
Grenada	11.4	0.8	0.7	0.6	0.6	0.9	1.4	1.9	2.6
St. Kitts and Nevis	0.0	0.0	0.0	0.0	0.0	0.0	0.0	0.3	1.1
St. Lucia	0.0	0.0	0.0	0.0	0.0	0.0	0.0	0.0	0.8
St. Vincent and the Grenadines	0.0	0.0	0.0	0.0	0.0	0.3	1.1	0.0	0.0
Total	179.8	203.9	241.9	265.1	301.5	333.8	331.6	314.6	342.4
Antigua and Barbuda	155.9	192.3	231.4	254.3	290.5	323.0	319.2	303.4	324.7
Dominica	0.0	0.6	0.7	1.0	1.1	2.0	1.9	0.9	0.5
Grenada	23.1	9.8	9.2	9.2	9.2	7.4	8.7	9.1	11.5
St. Kitts and Nevis	0.0	0.0	0.1	0.2	0.4	0.4	0.5	0.8	1.6
St. Lucia	0.5	1.2	0.3	0.1	0.1	0.1	0.2	0.2	4.1
St. Vincent and the Grenadines	0.1	0.0	0.2	0.1	0.1	0.9	1.1	0.2	0.0

Sources: Eastern Caribbean Central Bank, and IMF staff estimates.

leum products, jewelry, watches, and clocks. List D applies to petroleum products in Belize, to rice in Antigua, Dominica, and Jamaica, and to medicines in the OECS and Belize. There are also conditional duty exemptions (CDEs), which are end-use defined and apply to machinery, equipment, and materials for food processing, almost all inputs for industrial activities, nearly all agricultural and mining inputs, and all inputs required for the initial establishment and extension of hotels. Each CARICOM member state can at its own discretion determine the range of exempted activities to be incorporated in its national tariff schedule and the extent of the duty exemption. In most cases, nearly all eligible activities are exempted and full duty exemption is granted. In addition to the regional provisions of the CDEs, most

Table 34. ECCB Area: Selected Banking System Indicators by Country
(Millions of Eastern Caribbean dollars)

	December 31								
	1990	1991	1992	1993	1994	1995	1996	1997	1998
Net foreign asstes	639.0	703.5	761.7	725.2	705.3	929.4	696.5	653.4	990.8
Central bank	530.2	562.8	718.7	707.0	685.4	818.2	758.8	815.8	953.2
Foreign assets	543.8	590.1	746.6	719.5	698.1	836.3	778.7	823.7	957.5
Foreign liabilities	13.7	27.3	28.0	12.5	12.8	18.1	19.9	7.9	4.3
Commercial banks[1]	108.8	140.6	43.1	18.2	19.9	111.2	−62.3	−162.3	37.6
Antigua and Barbuda	−40.6	14.9	−14.9	13.1	52.3	74.3	25.7	−25.5	6.7
Dominica	3.3	−3.3	−0.9	−9.3	−16.4	−13.6	8.9	9.9	30.8
Grenada	−11.5	−8.4	−22.5	−20.8	−2.0	19.2	4.3	−42.6	−59.9
St. Kitts and Nevis	36.3	35.0	22.0	47.2	3.7	25.0	−35.2	−52.4	35.9
St. Lucia	38.6	38.2	35.1	−17.4	−52.0	−54.7	−105.4	−88.6	−78.8
St. Vincent and the Grenadines	72.4	69.6	41.3	26.1	19.0	8.5	−19.0	−30.8	0.9
Anguilla and Montserrat	10.3	−5.3	−17.0	−20.7	15.3	52.3	58.5	67.7	101.9
Domestic credit	2,169.7	2,387.3	2,567.0	2,891.0	2,992.3	3,299.8	3,651.8	4,135.6	4,434.0
Of which:									
Private sector	2,210.3	2,447.0	2,733.4	3,051.8	3,171.1	3,498.1	3,923.8	4,443.9	4,799.0
Antigua and Barbuda	503.1	547.4	607.1	625.3	613.8	706.9	850.3	1,027.0	1,103.2
Dominica	211.1	234.4	264.0	289.6	312.5	344.6	358.5	386.3	410.0
Grenada	270.7	287.5	315.0	413.6	414.6	437.3	495.3	588.0	684.7
St. Kitts and Nevis	231.8	262.5	334.3	375.8	416.4	440.9	464.9	521.1	563.7
St. Lucia	578.5	623.8	680.1	806.5	860.4	946.4	1,071.3	1,171.8	1,258.2
St. Vincent and the Grenadines	204.3	238.7	258.4	266.0	285.1	347.0	398.8	447.2	486.4
Anguilla and Montserrat	210.7	252.7	274.4	275.0	268.3	275.1	284.7	302.5	295.4
Nonfinancial public enterprises (net)	−293.7	−327.6	−332.1	−341.0	−383.1	−424.8	−474.2	−502.7	−570.9
Antigua and Barbuda	−24.6	−34.2	−44.0	−41.4	−56.8	−26.0	−40.1	−45.9	−30.5
Dominica	−1.0	4.5	−5.3	−3.0	−8.2	−17.3	−29.7	−27.0	−14.3
Grenada	5.6	4.1	1.3	−8.9	−19.7	−25.1	−24.6	−20.7	−24.8
St. Kitts and Nevis	−36.9	−49.9	−70.6	−80.0	−91.0	−95.5	−90.2	−91.7	−139.4
St. Lucia	−127.9	−137.8	−109.0	−99.6	−100.1	−112.8	−125.9	−134.7	−171.3
St. Vincent and the Grenadines	−90.8	−92.6	−77.4	−81.7	−74.2	−110.3	−121.0	−137.3	−148.3
Anguilla and Montserrat	−18.1	−21.7	−27.0	−26.5	−33.2	−37.7	−42.7	−45.4	−42.4
Central government (net)	358.0	378.3	320.9	347.1	340.3	410.9	452.3	451.0	456.4
Central bank credit (net)	155.2	158.0	117.0	115.5	106.5	85.6	91.2	76.0	56.5
Commercial bank credit (net)	202.8	220.3	204.0	231.7	233.8	325.3	361.1	375.0	399.9
Of which:									
Antigua and Barbuda	81.6	73.4	85.4	109.4	111.6	137.1	141.1	178.8	211.9
Dominica	12.6	25.2	30.6	33.8	39.1	51.0	59.1	62.6	41.0
Grenada	30.4	39.5	19.8	26.9	29.4	31.0	40.6	60.1	57.9
St. Kitts and Nevis	53.3	65.2	63.6	52.1	46.6	77.9	111.5	80.7	124.2
St. Lucia	−0.6	0.3	−25.2	−23.5	−26.9	−34.1	−39.8	−37.3	−51.1
St. Vincent and the Grenadines	28.2	18.7	27.6	35.7	37.4	66.2	58.7	55.1	38.6
Anguilla and Montserrat	−2.6	−2.0	2.2	−2.7	−3.5	−3.8	−10.1	−24.9	−22.6
Monetary liabilities (M2)	2,449.6	2,662.9	2,868.2	3,145.4	3,392.7	3,871.8	3,945.9	4,322.8	4,862.0
Of which:									
Commercial bank liabilities to the private sector	2,204.3	2,409.0	2,595.4	2,875.3	3,109.7	3,562.8	3,650.1	4,010.0	4,517.5
Antigua and Barbuda	506.3	587.5	623.3	687.7	757.2	921.6	880.9	963.6	1,107.8
Dominica	196.9	232.8	266.1	254.1	268.8	331.8	339.6	352.7	378.0
Grenada	290.6	305.7	329.7	407.4	451.6	496.9	547.6	613.2	686.4
St. Kitts and Nevis	257.8	265.1	310.1	346.8	361.8	408.1	430.3	493.2	510.1
St. Lucia	521.1	568.8	576.2	640.2	683.5	743.3	762.2	819.0	918.9
St. Vincent and the Grenadines	227.5	236.4	266.5	298.1	314.3	345.1	363.0	411.1	479.6
Anguilla and Montserrat	204.1	212.8	223.4	241.0	272.5	316.1	326.5	357.3	436.7

Source: Eastern Caribbean Central Bank.
[1]Country aggregates exclude balances held with other ECCB territories for the purpose of area-wide consolidation.

IV RECENT ECONOMIC DEVELOPMENTS

Table 35. ECCB Area: Sectoral Distribution of Commercial Banks' Loans and Advances

	December 31								
	1990[1]	1991	1992	1993	1994	1995	1996	1997	1998
	(Millions of Eastern Caribbean dollars)								
Total loans and advances	2,541.6	2,877.5	3,180.6	3,544.6	3,766.3	4,232.4	4,760.8	5,343.3	5,898.6
Agriculture	79.8	88.4	99.9	114.0	137.4	134.4	145.4	158.6	181.5
Fisheries	6.8	5.9	7.3	5.9	6.7	7.4	7.5	9.8	7.8
Manufacturing[2]	134.8	152.4	161.3	171.3	177.2	199.4	215.3	219.6	209.6
Utilities	55.7	63.9	109.9	100.2	98.1	82.9	107.2	113.7	128.7
Construction and land development	172.3	198.2	210.3	182.0	171.5	225.8	254.3	280.1	295.0
Distributive trades	369.3	412.9	465.5	534.8	566.2	625.2	668.4	730.2	755.0
Tourism	268.2	279.0	310.6	353.1	369.9	394.4	447.6	456.2	457.0
Entertainment and catering	24.8	27.5	38.7	39.5	39.4	49.5	64.2	63.8	76.1
Transportation and storage	111.6	104.4	106.2	107.0	108.6	138.7	144.1	163.6	158.3
Financial institutions	27.0	31.4	26.0	20.0	38.4	53.3	50.1	61.7	86.9
Professional and other services	76.6	81.1	130.1	156.5	161.7	209.4	234.9	289.7	311.7
Government services	232.5	235.2	243.5	269.2	292.9	395.6	431.7	472.5	570.7
Personal	982.2	1,197.1	1,271.4	1,491.3	1,598.3	1,716.4	1,989.9	2,323.9	2,660.2
Acquisition of property	541.4	653.9	712.1	824.8	928.9	1,015.7	1,185.9	1,308.7	1,401.6
Durable consumer goods	174.7	192.2	186.6	194.1	180.9	207.3	234.5	264.7	401.0
Other personal loans	266.1	351.0	372.7	472.3	488.5	493.5	569.5	750.5	857.6
	(Percent)								
Total loans and advances	100.0	100.0	100.0	100.0	100.0	100.0	100.0	100.0	100.0
Agriculture	3.1	3.1	3.1	3.2	3.6	3.2	3.1	3.0	3.1
Fisheries	0.3	0.2	0.2	0.2	0.2	0.2	0.2	0.2	0.1
Manufacturing[2]	5.3	5.3	5.1	4.8	4.7	4.7	4.5	4.1	3.6
Utilities	2.2	2.2	3.5	2.8	2.6	2.0	2.3	2.1	2.2
Construction and land development	6.8	6.9	6.6	5.1	4.6	5.3	5.3	5.2	5.0
Distributive trades	14.5	14.3	14.6	15.1	15.0	14.8	14.0	13.7	12.8
Tourism	10.6	9.7	9.8	10.0	9.8	9.3	9.4	8.5	7.7
Entertainment and catering	1.0	1.0	1.2	1.1	1.0	1.2	1.3	1.2	1.3
Transportation and storage	4.4	3.6	3.3	3.0	2.9	3.3	3.0	3.1	2.7
Financial institutions	1.1	1.1	0.8	0.6	1.0	1.3	1.1	1.2	1.5
Professional and other services	3.0	2.8	4.1	4.4	4.3	4.9	4.9	5.4	5.3
Government services	9.1	8.2	7.7	7.6	7.8	9.3	9.1	8.8	9.7
Personal	38.6	41.6	40.0	42.1	42.4	40.6	41.8	43.5	45.1
Acquisition of property	21.3	22.7	22.4	23.3	24.7	24.0	24.9	24.5	23.8
Durable consumer goods	6.9	6.7	5.9	5.5	4.8	4.9	4.9	5.0	6.8
Other personal loans	10.5	12.2	11.7	13.3	13.0	11.7	12.0	14.0	14.5

Source: Eastern Caribbean Central Bank.
[1] Does not include Montserrat as breakdown is not available. Therefore, total loans and advances and overdrafts will not match that of the balance sheet for the ECCB area.
[2] Includes mining and quarrying.

CARICOM countries exempt public sector enterprises from paying duty on imported inputs.

Nontariff barriers are widespread in the region. In particular, import licenses are widely used, as Article 56 of the CARICOM Agreement allows protection of domestic production from competition by more advanced CARICOM countries.[39] In addition, countries maintain licensing requirements to import a broad range of products from outside CARICOM. There are still some import quotas in place, including on beer in St. Kitts and Nevis. In all, trade restrictiveness effectively appears to be moderate in most of the countries (Table 41).

Countries in the region traditionally have run large current account deficits, compared to other, larger developing countries. The combined current account

---

[39] As allowed by Article 56 of the CARICOM Agreement, the OECS countries have imposed license requirements for imports from more advanced CARICOM countries on the following products: curry powder, wheat flour, pasta products, aerated beverages, beer, oxygen, carbon dioxide, acetylene, candles, solar water heaters, wood chairs, and other wood furniture.

Table 36. ECCB Area: Commercial Banks' Overdrafts and Loans by Maturity

	1990	1991	1992	1993	1994	1995	1996	1997	1998
	(Millions of Eastern Caribbean dollars)								
Overdrafts	741.2	817.6	860.8	909.8	972.8	1,080.3	1,147.3	1,092.6	1,198.4
Total loans	1,800.4	2,059.9	2,319.9	2,634.7	2,793.5	3,152.1	3,613.5	4,250.7	4,700.1
Up to 1 year	164.6	163.9	206.4	273.6	184.8	208.1	223.3	302.7	347.5
1 to 5 years	682.9	777.8	874.0	938.1	975.3	1,080.9	1,137.8	1,339.3	1,456.1
Over 5 years	952.9	1,118.3	1,239.5	1,423.0	1,633.3	1,863.3	2,252.4	2,608.7	2,896.6
Total loans and overdrafts	2,541.6	2,877.5	3,180.6	3,544.6	3,766.3	4,232.4	4,760.8	5,343.3	5,898.6
	(As a percentage of total loans and overdrafts)								
Overdrafts	29.2	28.4	27.1	25.7	25.8	25.5	24.1	20.4	20.3
Total loans	70.8	71.6	72.9	74.3	74.2	74.5	75.9	79.6	79.7
Up to 1 year	6.5	5.7	6.5	7.7	4.9	4.9	4.7	5.7	5.9
1 to 5 years	26.9	27.0	27.5	26.5	25.9	25.5	23.9	25.1	24.7
Over 5 years	37.5	38.9	39.0	40.1	43.4	44.0	47.3	48.8	49.1

Source: Eastern Caribbean Central Bank.

[1] Does not include Montserrat as breakdown is not available. Therefore, total loans and advances and overdrafts will not match that of the balance sheet for the ECCB area.

Table 37. ECCB Area: Selected Monetary Indicators

	December 31								
	1990	1991	1992	1993	1994	1995	1996	1997	1998
	(Annual changes as a percentage of beginning of period M2)								
Net foreign assets	0.4	2.6	2.2	−1.3	−0.6	6.6	−6.0	−1.1	7.8
Central bank (net)	2.6	1.3	5.9	−0.4	−0.7	3.9	−1.5	1.4	3.2
Commercial banks (net)	−2.2	1.3	−3.7	−0.9	0.1	2.7	−4.5	−2.5	4.6
Domestic credit (net)	10.6	8.9	6.7	11.3	3.2	9.0	9.1	12.3	6.9
Of which:									
To private sector	11.0	9.7	10.8	11.1	3.8	9.6	11.0	13.2	8.3
To central government (net)	1.3	0.8	−2.2	0.9	−0.2	2.1	1.1	0.0	0.1
To nonfinancial public enterprises (net)	−1.3	−1.4	−0.2	−0.3	−1.3	−1.2	−1.3	−0.7	−1.6
Monetary liabilities (M2)	10.1	8.7	7.7	9.7	7.9	14.1	1.9	9.6	12.5
Other items (net)	−0.8	−2.8	−1.2	−0.4	5.3	−1.5	−1.2	−1.6	−2.3
	(Percent)								
Memorandum items:									
Ratios to GDP									
M2	54.2	55.8	56.0	59.2	60.0	66.1	63.8	66.8	71.8
Quasi-money	41.2	43.4	42.0	45.2	46.0	50.6	49.6	51.9	55.7
As a ratio of liabilities to the private sector									
Currency held by the public	10.0	9.5	9.5	8.6	8.3	8.0	7.5	7.2	7.1
Demand deposits	14.0	12.6	15.5	15.1	15.0	15.5	14.8	15.0	15.3
Time deposits	28.2	28.9	26.5	24.4	22.6	23.2	22.6	23.0	24.0
Savings deposits	41.5	42.0	41.3	44.4	46.3	44.9	46.3	44.8	43.8
Foreign currency deposits	6.2	7.0	7.2	7.5	7.7	8.4	8.8	9.9	9.8

Source: Eastern Caribbean Central Bank.

IV RECENT ECONOMIC DEVELOPMENTS

Table 38. ECCB Area: Effective Exchange Rates
(1990 = 100)

	Antigua and Barbuda		Dominica		Grenada		St. Kitts and Nevis		St. Lucia		St. Vincent and the Grenadines	
	Nominal	Real	Nominal	Real	Nominal	Real	Nominal	Real	Nominal	Real	Nominal	Real
I. Average												
1980	93.7	104.2	72.3	90.9	77.3	91.7	83.8	109.8	83.9	101.7	80.5	101.0
1981	97.3	109.1	76.9	98.2	83.4	106.1	87.4	113.4	88.8	111.6	84.4	106.8
1982	101.7	110.6	82.0	101.5	88.8	112.6	91.5	116.4	93.8	114.5	88.5	110.6
1983	105.0	111.6	88.6	108.0	93.7	118.7	95.4	117.7	98.8	116.3	92.4	114.6
1984	110.1	115.5	101.2	116.9	100.5	126.6	100.5	120.0	106.7	121.8	97.2	116.4
1985	112.4	114.0	107.5	120.2	103.3	126.7	102.6	119.5	110.3	120.3	99.3	115.3
1986	107.6	106.4	101.4	111.5	98.9	118.0	102.6	115.4	104.9	113.1	100.1	113.4
1987	103.4	102.1	96.5	107.2	93.6	106.1	99.9	108.3	100.1	110.9	97.5	108.2
1988	100.4	101.6	93.2	100.8	91.4	103.1	97.7	101.3	97.1	103.9	95.6	101.6
1989	103.4	102.6	97.5	105.0	96.3	107.7	101.7	103.6	100.7	105.8	100.0	102.5
1990	100.0	100.0	100.0	100.0	100.0	100.0	100.0	100.0	100.0	100.0	100.0	100.0
1991	101.2	101.8	104.2	101.7	108.2	99.2	100.1	99.6	103.4	102.2	104.0	102.2
1992	101.2	100.4	108.2	102.6	117.3	98.3	99.3	98.3	105.5	102.9	106.5	100.7
1993	107.5	106.6	118.0	105.6	139.4	103.8	103.3	101.1	116.8	106.9	118.6	107.7
1994	107.6	106.8	123.6	101.8	159.3	103.7	103.2	99.9	122.2	106.3	125.0	104.8
1995	104.2	103.5	119.9	95.9	157.6	100.2	100.8	97.7	118.4	105.1	120.9	99.7
1996	105.8	105.1	123.4	97.2	161.0	101.4	102.1	98.4	120.9	105.6	124.1	103.9
1997	109.1	109.0	130.6	102.6	167.6	104.2	104.6	107.0	126.6	108.1	131.4	107.6
1998	110.1	111.2	138.5	107.6	170.1	105.3	105.6	109.9	129.1	111.1	135.9	111.4
1999¹	111.2	113.6	137.2	106.6	173.9	105.8	105.8	112.7	130.7	116.7	137.3	110.9
II. End of Period												
1990 Dec.	96.5	97.6	98.4	99.9	100.7	96.9	97.4	96.7	97.5	96.3	97.8	98.4
1991 Dec.	100.0	99.7	105.0	100.0	110.3	96.4	98.6	98.7	102.5	101.5	103.3	99.3
1992 Dec.	105.0	104.1	113.0	104.5	126.4	101.2	101.7	100.4	111.1	105.9	112.1	103.1
1993 Dec.	109.6	108.7	123.1	106.6	151.5	106.7	104.6	101.9	121.9	108.2	124.4	109.7
1994 Dec.	106.7	106.0	123.2	99.5	161.0	102.4	102.6	98.5	121.8	107.6	124.6	103.2
1995 Dec.	105.2	104.5	121.6	96.3	159.4	100.1	101.5	97.8	119.5	107.4	122.2	101.2
1996 Dec.	105.4	104.8	124.3	97.6	161.6	101.9	102.1	98.6	121.1	103.5	125.0	104.2
1997 Dec.	110.0	110.4	138.8	108.6	169.6	105.4	105.4	110.9	129.1	110.1	135.7	111.2
1998 Dec.	108.2	109.9	133.6	104.4	167.1	103.0	104.2	108.8	126.1	110.6	132.3	109.8
1999 Dec.	112.2	114.8	137.1	105.2	175.0	105.5	106.1	112.0	131.9	120.2	138.5	109.7

Source: IMF Information Notice System.
¹Data refer to the period January–October 1999.

Figure 1. ECCB Area: Exchange Rate Developments, 1981–99
(1990 = 100)

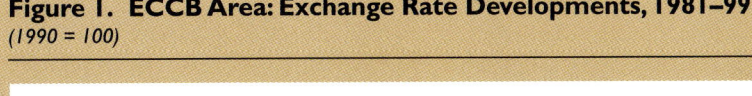

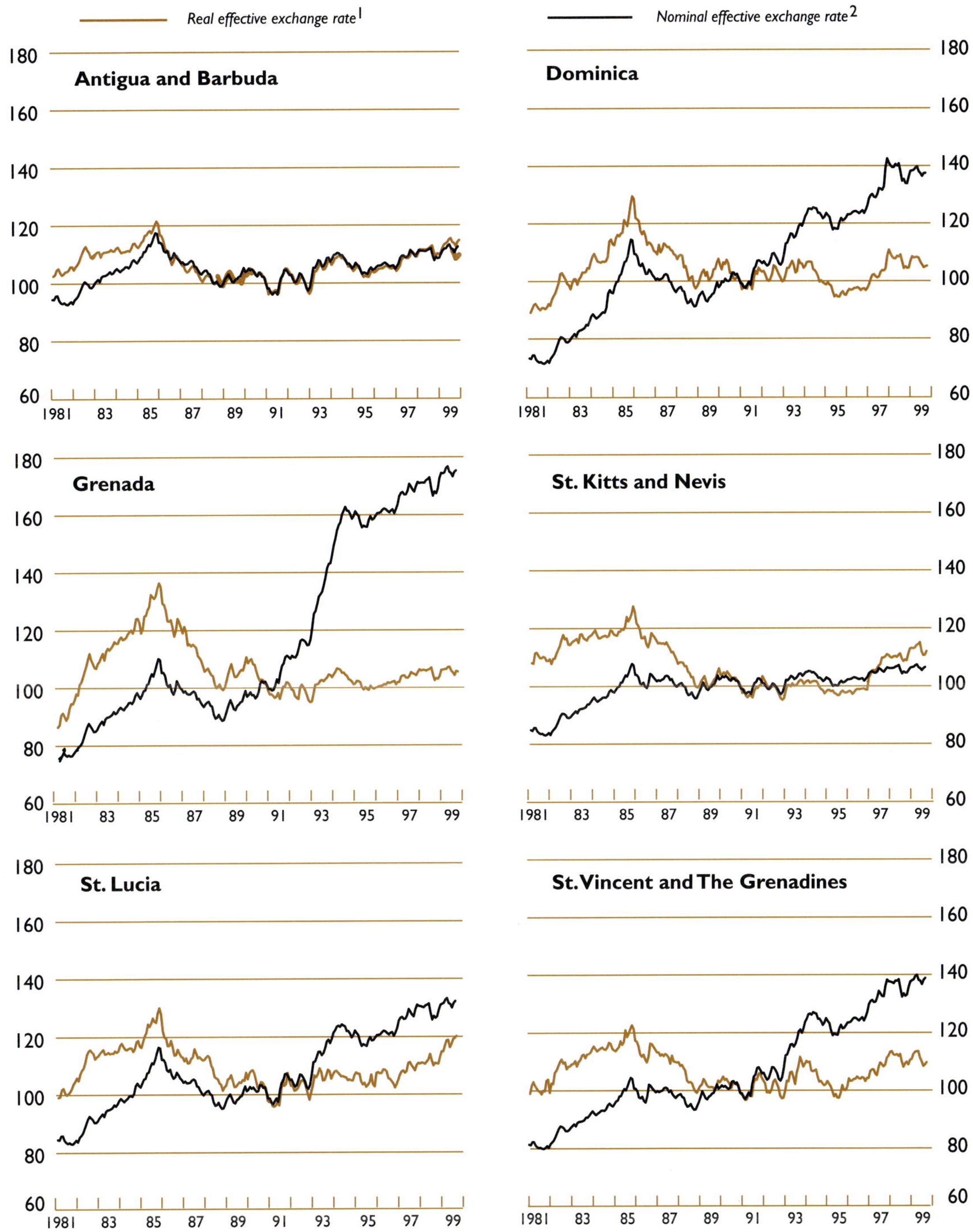

Source: IMF Information Notice System.
[1] IMF trade-weighted index of nominal exchange rates deflated by seasonally-adjusted relative consumer prices; increase means appreciation.
[2] Seasonally adjusted.

IV RECENT ECONOMIC DEVELOPMENTS

Table 39. CARICOM: Implementation of Scheduled Reductions in the Maximum Rate of the Common External Tariff[1]

Phases of implementation	I	II	III	IV
Period of application	Jan. 1, 1993–Dec. 31, 1994	Jan. 1, 1995–Dec. 31, 1996	Jan. 1–Dec. 31, 1997	Jan. 1, 1998 and beyond
Maximum rate	35	30	25	20
Scheduled period for implementation	Jan.–June 1993	Jan.–June 1995	Jan.–June 1997	Jan.–June 1998
Antigua and Barbuda	Completed January 2, 1995	Not implemented	Not implemented	Planned for January, 2000
Barbados	Completed April 1, 1993	Completed April 1, 1995	Completed April 1, 1997	Completed April 1, 1998
Belize[2]	...	Completed April 1, 1997	Completed April 1, 1998	Planned for April 1, 2000
Dominica	Completed September 1, 1993	Completed October 1, 1995	Completed January 1, 1999	Not implemented
Grenada	Completed July 1, 1993	Completed June 30, 1995	Completed July 1, 1997	Completed January 15, 2000
Guyana	Completed January 14, 1994	Completed September 5, 1995	Completed November 1, 1997	Completed April 30, 1999
Jamaica[3]	Completed April 1, 1993	Completed April 1, 1993	Completed January 1, 1995	Completed January, 1999
St. Kitts and Nevis	Completed July 5, 1993	Completed January 1, 1995	Not implemented	Not implemented
St. Lucia	Completed July 1, 1993	Completed July 1, 1997	Not implemented	Completed January 1, 2000
St. Vincent and the Grenadines	Completed April 2, 1993	Completed January 1, 1996	Completed January 1, 1997	Completed January 1, 1998
Suriname[4]	...	Completed January 1, 1996	Completed July 1, 1997	Planned for July, 2000
Trinidad and Tobago	Completed January 1, 1993	Completed January 1, 1996	Completed January 1, 1997	Completed July 1, 1998

Source: CARICOM Secretariat.

[1] The CET excludes agricultural products, which are subject to a rate of 40 percent.
[2] Belize has been granted permission to implement each phase with a two-year lag.
[3] For phase I, the maximum rate was lowered to 30 percent. For phase II, the maximum rate was lowered to 25 percent.
[4] Joined the Caribbean Common Market in 1996.

Table 40. CARICOM: Common External Tariff Rates

	January 1, 1993–December 31, 1994	January 1, 1995–December 31, 1996	January 1, 1997–December 31, 1997	From January 1, 1998
Agricultural inputs	0	0	0	0
Noncompeting primary inputs	5 (LDCs 0–5)	5 (LDCs 0–5)	5 (LDCs 0–5)	5 (LDCs 0–5)
Noncompeting intermediate inputs	5 (LDCs 0–5)	5 (LDCs 0–5)	5 (LDCs 0–5)	5 (LDCs 0–5)
Noncompeting capital inputs	5 (LDCs 0–5)	5 (LDCs 0–5)	5 (LDCs 0–5)	5 (LDCs 0–5)
Competing primary inputs	20	15	10	10
Competing capital goods	20	15	10	10
Selected imports	20	15	10	10
Competing intermediate inputs	25	20	15	15
Noncompeting final goods	25	25–30	20–25	20
Agro-industry	30–35	25–30	20–25	20
Garments	30–35	25–30	20–25	20
General manufactures	30–35	25–30	20–25	20
Agriculture	40	40	40	40

Source: Caricom Secretariat.

Table 41. ECCB Area: Statutory Tax Rates on International Trade and Transactions
(as of December 1999)

	Anguilla	Antigua and Barbuda	Dominica	Grenada	Montserrat	St. Kitts and Nevis	St. Lucia	St. Vincent and the Grenadines
Import tariff (In percent)[1]	5–35	0–70	0–40	0–40	5–30	0–70	0–70	0–40
Average tariff rate (In percent)[2]	...	9.7	10.1	10.5	...	9.6	10.4	9.8
Custom service charge (in percent)	None	5.0	1.0	5.0	8.0	3.0	4.0	2.5
Index of trade restrictiveness[3]	...	5.0	5.0	9.0	...	2.0	5.0	5.0

Sources: Eastern Caribbean Central Bank, Inter-American Development Bank, and IMF staff estimates.
[1] Consistent with the CARICOM agreement, agricultural inputs are duty free and agricultural products are subject to duties of up to 40 percent.
[2] Defined as the simple average of the statutory rates.
[3] The index value ranges between one and ten, with one representing the least restrictive trade regime. The index has been calculated on the basis of numerous factors, including the minimum and maximum tariff rates, the number of bands, the allocation of individual items to the bands, existence of "exceptional" rates that lie outside the basic tariff structure, any other duties and charges (such as differential rates of excise or VAT taxes on imports, import surcharges, and statistical fees), and the extent of customs duty exemptions. It also takes into account the production or trade coverage of nontariff barriers.

deficit of the region averaged 13½ percent of GDP during 1990–98 (Table 42), with certain countries recording deficits of 20 percent of GDP or higher on occasion (Table 43). Preliminary information points to a combined deficit of around 16 percent in 1999, little changed from the 1997–98 level. Apart from periodic changes in countries' current account deficits caused by hurricanes and other natural disasters, public and private investment projects (construction of hotels, public utilities, roads, and other infrastructure) tend to raise imports to very high levels for short periods. Such additional imports are financed from the accompanying flows of direct investment or loans and grants to the public sector.

IV RECENT ECONOMIC DEVELOPMENTS

Table 42. ECCB Area: Summary Balance of Payments[1]

	1990	1991	1992	1993	1994	1995	1996	1997	1998
	(Millions of U.S. dollars)								
Current account	−282.9	−294.2	−200.6	−210.0	−230.1	−211.1	−330.6	−387.3	−407.9
Goods and nonfactor services	−233.9	−246.9	−155.1	−156.8	−182.2	−257.4	−325.8	−353.9	−404.4
Goods	−608.0	−667.0	−619.4	−678.5	−762.3	−767.0	−849.1	−938.3	−995.0
Exports	365.3	343.0	384.5	349.5	299.5	354.5	336.5	303.8	323.0
Imports	973.3	1010.0	1003.9	1027.9	1061.8	1121.5	1185.5	1242.1	1318.0
Nonfactor services (net)	374.1	420.1	464.3	521.6	580.1	509.7	523.3	584.4	590.6
Travel	484.3	524.5	584.5	658.6	730.9	689.9	710.4	768.7	776.7
Transportation	−86.8	−70.9	−75.6	−81.5	−83.9	−89.9	−98.2	−102.1	−117.7
Other[2]	−23.4	−33.6	−44.6	−55.5	−66.8	−90.3	−88.9	−82.2	−68.3
Net factor income	−113.7	−102.1	−98.0	−103.4	−117.4	−124.6	−128.1	−137.7	−156.2
Investment income	−109.7	−102.5	−98.3	−103.5	−117.5	−124.1	−126.9	−135.6	−155.6
Other	−4.1	0.4	0.3	0.0	0.1	−0.5	−1.2	−2.1	−0.6
Current transfers (net)	64.8	54.7	52.5	50.3	69.4	170.8	123.3	104.3	152.7
Capital and financial account	336.9	284.5	273.9	201.4	225.0	225.7	342.2	426.1	392.7
Capital account (net)	66.9	69.8	55.6	51.2	58.3	78.7	73.5	100.3	136.7
Capital transfers	66.9	69.8	55.6	51.2	57.6	67.0	69.4	100.3	136.7
Other	0.0	0.0	0.0	0.0	0.7	11.8	4.0	0.0	0.0
Financial account (net)	270.0	214.7	218.3	150.2	166.7	146.9	268.7	325.7	256.0
Direct investment	208.0	187.4	151.0	138.8	180.1	207.6	183.5	225.7	260.4
Portfolio investment	−0.3	0.0	−0.7	2.4	−2.0	−7.1	3.4	0.0	0.2
Other	62.3	27.4	68.0	8.9	−11.4	−53.6	81.8	100.1	−4.6
Of which:									
Public sector capital	48.0	43.8	40.3	15.7	18.5	3.1	15.9	61.6	28.2
Commercial banks	28.8	−9.9	32.1	−17.8	−20.4	−31.9	60.9	37.8	−58.9
Net errors and omissions	−33.5	22.7	−20.5	4.1	12.7	26.8	−26.5	−14.7	71.7
Overall balance	20.5	12.9	52.8	−4.5	7.6	41.4	−14.9	24.0	56.5
	(Percent of GDP)								
Current account	−16.9	−16.6	−10.6	−10.7	−11.0	−9.7	−14.4	−16.0	−15.8
Goods and nonfactor services	−14.0	−14.0	−8.2	−8.0	−8.7	−11.8	−14.2	−14.7	−15.7
Goods	−36.3	−37.7	−32.6	−34.4	−36.3	−35.2	−37.0	−38.8	−38.6
Exports	21.8	19.4	20.3	17.7	14.3	16.3	14.7	12.6	12.5
Imports	58.1	57.1	52.9	52.2	50.6	51.5	51.7	51.4	51.1
Nonfactor services (net)	22.3	23.7	24.5	26.5	27.6	23.4	22.8	24.2	22.9
Travel	28.9	29.7	30.8	33.4	34.8	31.7	31.0	31.8	30.1
Transportation	−5.2	−4.0	−4.0	−4.1	−4.0	−4.1	−4.3	−4.2	−4.6
Other[2]	−1.4	−1.9	−2.4	−2.8	−3.2	−4.2	−3.9	−3.4	−2.6
Net factor income	−6.8	−5.8	−5.2	−5.3	−5.6	−5.7	−5.6	−5.7	−6.1
Investment income	−6.6	−5.8	−5.2	−5.3	−5.6	−5.7	−5.5	−5.6	−6.0
Other	−0.2	0.0	0.0	0.0	0.0	0.0	−0.1	−0.1	0.0
Current transfers (net)	3.9	3.1	2.8	2.6	3.3	7.8	5.4	4.3	5.9
Capital and financial account	20.1	16.1	14.4	10.2	10.7	10.4	14.9	17.6	15.2
Capital account (net)	4.0	3.9	2.9	2.6	2.8	3.6	3.2	4.2	5.3
Capital transfers	4.0	3.9	2.9	2.6	2.7	3.1	3.0	4.2	5.3
Other	0.0	0.0	0.0	0.0	0.0	0.5	0.2	0.0	0.0
Financial account (net)	16.1	12.1	11.5	7.6	7.9	6.8	11.7	13.5	9.9
Direct investment	12.4	10.6	8.0	7.0	8.6	9.5	8.0	9.3	10.1
Portfolio investment	0.0	0.0	0.0	0.1	−0.1	−0.3	0.1	0.0	0.0
Other	3.7	1.5	3.6	0.5	−0.5	−2.5	3.6	4.1	−0.2
Of which:									
Public sector capital	2.9	2.5	2.1	0.8	0.9	0.1	0.7	2.5	1.1
Commercial banks	1.7	−0.6	1.7	−0.9	−1.0	−1.5	2.7	1.6	−2.3
Net errors and omissions	−2.0	1.3	−1.1	0.2	0.6	1.2	−1.2	−0.6	2.8
Overall balance	1.2	0.7	2.8	−0.2	0.4	1.9	−0.6	1.0	2.2

Sources: Eastern Caribbean Central Bank, and IMF staff estimates.
[1]The area includes Anguilla and Montserrat.
[2]Includes insurance, financial, other business, and government services, and storage and bunkers.

Table 43. ECCB Area: Current Account by Country

	1990	1991	1992	1993	1994	1995	1996	1997	1998
	(Millions of U.S. dollars)								
ECCB area	−282.9	−294.2	−200.6	−210.0	−230.1	−211.1	−330.6	−387.3	−407.9
Anguilla	−8.5	−7.3	−16.7	−12.8	−11.4	−9.4	−20.2	−18.8	−10.9
Antigua and Barbuda	−31.0	−33.5	−18.9	−0.5	−17.9	−0.5	−70.9	−64.4	−97.3
Dominica	−43.7	−34.3	−25.3	−22.6	−38.4	−45.6	−39.9	−33.6	−18.3
Grenada	−46.0	−46.2	−32.2	−43.6	−27.3	−41.0	−57.8	−69.3	−90.6
Montserrat	−23.0	−19.6	−12.7	−7.6	−11.9	−2.6	13.7	−2.1	−16.8
St. Kitts and Nevis	−47.8	−36.0	−15.5	−29.3	−23.3	−45.1	−68.3	−55.2	−44.4
St. Lucia	−58.3	−72.1	−55.1	−49.6	−41.6	−26.3	−55.5	−80.0	−67.1
St. Vincent and the Grenadines	−24.5	−45.2	−24.1	−44.0	−58.2	−40.7	−31.5	−63.9	−62.7
	(Percent of GDP)								
ECCB area	−16.9	−16.6	−10.6	−10.7	−11.0	−9.7	−14.4	−16.0	−15.8
Anguilla	−15.6	−13.1	−27.5	−19.3	−15.4	−12.5	−25.6	−21.2	−11.4
Antigua and Barbuda	−7.9	−8.2	−4.5	−0.1	−3.6	−0.1	−13.1	−11.1	−15.6
Dominica	−26.3	−19.0	−13.2	−11.3	−17.8	−20.5	−16.9	−13.8	−7.1
Grenada	−20.8	−19.1	−12.8	−17.4	−10.4	−14.9	−19.6	−22.0	−27.0
Montserrat	−34.3	−35.2	−21.7	−12.3	−18.7	−4.3	28.1	−5.7	−47.1
St. Kitts and Nevis	−30.0	−21.9	−8.5	−14.8	−10.5	−19.5	−27.8	−20.1	−15.4
St. Lucia	−14.0	−16.1	−11.1	−10.0	−8.0	−4.7	−9.7	−13.8	−10.7
St. Vincent and the Grenadines	−12.3	−21.3	−10.3	−18.4	−23.9	−15.4	−11.3	−21.7	−19.8

Sources: Eastern Caribbean Central Bank, and IMF staff estimates.

The persistent problems affecting the banana sector (described above) have contributed to the recent deterioration in the region's export performance. As banana export volume fell by half from 1990 to 1998, regional banana export earnings declined by about 50 percent and the share of banana exports in total merchandise exports dropped markedly. In relation to total exports of goods and services, the decline in banana exports (from 13 percent to 4⅓ percent) was broadly offset by the rise in tourism earnings.

Capital flows into the region during 1990–98 were sufficient to finance the deficits on current account and to permit an accumulation of official reserves held by the ECCB (see Table 42). Direct investment is the single largest source of capital inflows to the region, averaging US$195 million a year during 1990–98 (or about 9½ percent of the regional GDP). Direct investment in individual countries shows considerable variation over time, as major projects are undertaken or completed. Grants and loans to the public sector are the other major source of long-term capital, averaging just above US$100 million a year during 1990–98.

V   Main Regional Policy Issues

The Currency Union Arrangement

The ECCB maintains open access to a common pool of foreign exchange and aims its credit policy at providing strong foreign exchange backing for currency issued, thereby supporting the fixed exchange rate policy. Under this arrangement, of course, there is no scope for monetary policy at the national level, the trend rate of inflation in the region is determined fundamentally by inflation in the United States and the other main trading partners, and market interest rates within the region follow closely world interest rates with a premium reflecting local conditions. While the region's trading systems have been relatively open by necessity, until recently the capital accounts have been relatively insulated from the rest of the world by restrictions and, perhaps, geographical isolation.

In practice, the ECCB operates as a quasi-currency board. It has maintained foreign exchange backing of close to 100 percent of monetary liabilities, well in excess of the minimum requirement of 60 percent set in the 1983 Act of Agreement. This has been possible because the 1983 Agreement stipulates that lending to governments, up to prescribed limits, is at the discretion of the ECCB, and because member governments have exercised restraint in borrowing from the ECCB.[40]

The ECCB management considers that the authorities in the region are satisfied with the currency union arrangement and with the price and exchange rate stability that it has facilitated. At the same time, there is awareness that to safeguard the arrangement and promote efficiency within the common currency area it is important to improve the flexibility of goods and factor markets, intensify efforts aimed at trade and capital liberalization, strengthen the banking system, and maintain fiscal discipline.

---

[40]As noted earlier, the stock of net ECCB credit to member governments declined during the 1990s.

Fiscal Policy

Fiscal policy in the region is conducted independently by each member country. In contrast to the recent experience with European Monetary Union, there have been no fiscal harmonization criteria or targets, but the common currency arrangement has fostered a tradition of fiscal discipline. However, there have been exceptions, with some countries including at times sizable fiscal deficits without recourse to ECCB credit by borrowing from external or domestic creditors. Moreover, in several countries in the region, public sector saving has remained low in recent years, frequently with adverse consequences for public investment and the growth of output and employment. At the same time, the banana producing countries are facing an urgent need to restructure, as continued access to protected markets is in question.

Economic size, trade liberalization, and incentives for economic development also pose challenges to fiscal policy. Policymakers note that diseconomies of small scale lead to high unit costs in general, and to relatively large wage bills in particular. The unit cost of providing public goods and operating separate customs and tax collection services are relatively high. Further trade liberalization is likely to result in a need to offset import tax revenue losses. Revenue performance remains hindered by an extensive array of tax concessions, with exemptions widely granted on taxes on business income and on imports under incentive regimes favoring manufacturing, tourism, and agricultural firms as well as other activities that qualify on social and economic grounds.

Against this backdrop, the main policy issues are the need to raise public saving and investment, improve the quality of public expenditure, strengthen government revenue, increase the institutional efficiency of the governments, and find ways to intensify regional cooperation. Some of these issues carry greater urgency for certain countries. In particular, St. Kitts and Nevis has been undertaking a substantial reconstruction effort in the wake of Hurricane Georges, and Dominica and St. Vincent and the

> **Box 7. Fiscal Reform Objectives and Measures Proposed by the ECCB**
>
> Raising central government saving to around 4–5 percent of GDP, and public sector saving to 7–8 percent of GDP.
>
> A tax reform to improve efficiency, equity, and buoyancy, in order to promote saving and investment and strengthen tax administration. Specific measures would include:
>
> - Harmonize the maximum rate for the personal and corporate income tax;
> - Exempt dividend and interest earnings from the personal income tax;
> - Broaden the tax base by introducing a tax on value-added, or a general consumption tax covering services with rebates on inputs for exports;
> - Eliminate the foreign exchange tax;
> - Adhere to CARICOM schedule for the implementation of the CET;
> - Extend the embarkation tax to seaport departures;
> - Preserve diversity in tax revenue by ensuring adequate balance between direct and indirect taxation;
> - Improve property valuation and registration, as well as the billing and collection of the property tax;
> - Streamline tax concessions;
> - Maintain the real value of licenses and government fees; and
> - Stricter application of penalties for tax crimes.
>
> Expenditure reform aimed at raising quality and efficiency by:
>
> - Improving budgeting procedures and practices and preparing multiyear budgets;
> - Tightening expenditure controls;
> - Better targeting of welfare programs;
> - Privatizing utilities where there are identifiable benefits;
> - Introducing regional procurement of selected goods and services, including education and health services, and foreign representation and negotiations;
> - Framing the public sector investment program (PSIP) in the context of an overall development strategy and in a manner consistent with absorptive capacity; and
> - Strengthening coordination in the preparation, implementation, and monitoring of the PSIP.
>
> Technical assistance and close collaboration with governments in financial programming and policy design. This would be complemented by the creation of a public sector database and by improved compilation of public sector statistics.

Grenadines are seeking to expand their airport facilities. Virtually all countries face the challenge of strengthening public saving in order to help fund needed improvements in infrastructure, particularly in view of the limited prospects for increased external grants.

The ECCB has put forward a proposal to its member governments to address these issues through the creation of fiscal regimes conducive to economic growth and development, social equity, and fiscal stability over the medium term (Box 7). The ECCB considers that an increase in public saving is needed to help fund increased public investment, provide adequate counterpart funds for externally supported projects, eliminate arrears, help amortize debt by constituting sinking funds, and create reserves against emergencies. The proposed fiscal reform program envisages public saving targets in the range of 4–5 percent of GDP for central governments and 7–8 percent for the public sector that would help cover public investment of 12 percent of GDP. The ECCB keeps these targets under review in case of changing conditions.

Under the program, the ECCB would help governments institutionalize financial programming as a tool for fiscal management and promote the allocation of central bank profits to building up fiscal reserves. To do this, it created in 1995 a two-tranche fiscal reserve facility, with the first tranche funded with portions of the profits that the ECCB distributes annually and that governments deposit, at their discretion, in facility accounts at the ECCB. These resources, however, are freely available to governments, thereby constituting short-term liabilities of the ECCB. Before distributing profits to governments, the ECCB allocates EC$4 million annually into the second tranche of this facility, maintaining these resources pooled in its reserves. Use of second tranche reserves has to be approved by the Monetary Council, as these resources have been earmarked as saving to be used only in a last resort case or to help deal with natural disasters. The ECCB's fiscal reform proposal calls for governments to raise public saving and deposit part of the increase into first tranche accounts. At the same time, the ECCB is proposing that governments forgo profit distributions, dedicating instead distributable profits to build up the fiscal reserve facility.

Governments are still to take ownership and adopt the ECCB proposals, or to set a timetable for imple-

V MAIN REGIONAL POLICY ISSUES

mentation. In addition, a few aspects of the fiscal reform plan deserve review. Ways to achieve the targeted public saving should be identified, with a clear determination of the mix of revenue and expenditure measures. There is also awareness of the need to update the size of the required adjustment and calibrate the proposed adjustment measures to ensure that they adequately fit the needs of each country. Finally, there is a question whether the proposed fiscal saving targets can be achieved without addressing the issue of the public sector wage bill, not only through wage moderation, but also through compensation system reform and downsizing of the civil service, including through regional consolidation of the provision of certain public services. There also ought to be consistency between saving targets and the expectations and conditionality increasingly set by donors (Box 8).

While the ratio of taxes to GDP is already high, there is considerable scope in most countries to improve the efficiency of the tax system. With the reductions in import duty collections resulting from trade liberalization, sentiment for the adoption of value-added taxation seems to be increasing, despite the administrative difficulties perceived with such systems in very small states. Both Dominica and Grenada are considering it and have received technical assistance from the IMF for this. The ECCB has prepared a position paper and has advised that VAT is an economically efficient tax. The ECCB recommends the introduction of VAT only if there is strong political backing and after the high administrative demands are adequately addressed. Regional harmonization in sensitive areas such as tax incentives has proven to be difficult, but harmonization of tax laws and regulations in other areas is proceeding, albeit slowly. A recent ECCB report assessing the revenue losses from tax incentives and exemptions in the member countries has drawn attention to this issue and has spurred St. Lucia to undertake a review of discretionary exemptions. There is also scope in all countries for reform of property taxes by linking them more closely to property values.

Monetary Issues

The Regional Government Securities Market

An important issue in the launching of the RGSM is the extent of ECCB involvement in the operations of the market. If the ECCB were to provide liquidity support in the event of undersold auctions, either directly as a "buyer of last resort" or indirectly through the commercial banks, the backing ratio could drop below its traditionally high levels. Thus, the integrity of the current quasi-currency board arrangement would be best preserved by avoiding the potential moral hazard problem that could ensue from providing governments with the incentive to issue more debt than they would otherwise, and shielding governments with unsound policies from the rigors of market assessment by allowing enlarged access to financing.

The ECCB's position regarding its likely activity in the RGSM is that it will only purchase unsold treasury bills in the primary market up to an amount that would effectively roll over its holdings of that country's government securities. This would help preserve the current level of the foreign exchange cover. That is, it will be prepared to access the primary auction to replace bills maturing at that time (and which would have been rolled over automatically in the absence of the RGSM). If the private demand is there, the ECCB would not replace bills and reduce its holdings. Preserving the existing holdings of bills, however, would require some reallocations should the three member states that do not presently issue government securities choose to enter the government securities market. Although the precise scope of the Bank's activity in the secondary market has not yet been defined, the principle has been established that acquisitions of securities through the secondary market will be temporary in nature, through auction-based agreements that call for repurchase before maturity.

The Interbank Market

Most interbank lending is believed to take place on a bilateral basis, at rates that are higher than the official interbank rate and vary depending on lenders' assessment of credit risk. Based on the loan amounts outstanding in the official interbank market and the outstanding amounts shown in the commercial banks' accounts due to and from banks in other ECCB territories, it can be estimated that over 90 percent of interbank trading takes place in the unofficial market. One possible explanation is the absence of a securitization requirement (which is particularly relevant given the shortage of eligible securities partly because of oversubscription of the central bank's rediscount window) in the unofficial market, where loans are essentially transacted on the basis of creditworthiness and guided by credit line limits. There are also indications that some liquidity-constrained commercial banks have made a practice of borrowing interbank funds in the unofficial market for periods in excess of 30 days, for the purpose of extending further credit.

The ECCB is presently discussing with the commercial banks a proposal to integrate the two markets that would allow the rate in the official market to be market determined. Under this proposal, the central bank would still help to minimize bank search and information costs by matching bids and offers, but current securitization requirements would be eliminated and the central bank would no longer guarantee interbank transactions. Market determination of the interbank rate is an important feature of ongoing money and capital markets reforms. Since the interbank rate is a critical factor affecting the cost of funds, its market determination should serve as a useful reference for interest rates in general. Moreover, the ECCB can encourage participation in the interbank market by maintaining its discount rate above the prevailing interbank rate, which would also serve as a cap on the interbank rate (see discussion below).

The Treasury Bill Rediscount Window

The ECCB's capacity to rediscount treasury bills is circumscribed by the legal limits on its holdings of each member's bills and its commitment to a high foreign exchange backing ratio. The present rediscount window is ordinarily "fully subscribed" owing to various market imperfections that discourage active commercial bank participation in the secondary treasury bill market. For instance, interest payments and redemptions of bills and debentures are sometimes delayed owing both to management inefficiency and occasional cash shortages in countries facing difficult fiscal positions. Since the ECCB guarantees the interest and principal payments of treasury bills that it rediscounts and the bills can be resold to the ECCB at the banks' discretion, these assets are, however, perfectly liquid and essentially risk-free for the commercial banks, which in turn routinely roll over their holdings. The appeal of these instruments to commercial banks is enhanced by a shortage of viable investment alternatives, owing partly to the tendency of many local banks to limit their investments to the home country, which is reinforced by several capital account restrictions. Oversubscription of the rediscount window constrains the ECCB's ability to tighten monetary conditions.

In order to strengthen credit policy, the ECCB plans to replace the existing treasury bill rediscount window with a market-based government securities repurchase (repo) auction as part of the introduction of the RGSM. This system would facilitate market determination of the rediscount rate, which would then better reflect prevailing liquidity conditions. A gradual phasing in would be a way to start this program, commencing with an initial auction of a small proportion (say 25 percent) of the current fixed rate facility. This proportion could then be increased steadily as and when the bills rediscounted through the existing rediscount window mature. Alternatively the new system could be initiated once all the existing bills mature, since they are short-term instruments.

The ECCB is also considering whether to transform the discount window into a Lombard Facility, with commercial banks being given only limited access (say, the equivalent of a bank's capital) to short-term loans (ranging in maturity from one to seven days) in the form of repurchase operations in treasury bills. The proposed Lombard Facility would serve as a useful complement to the reforms proposed in the interbank market, as banks would have direct recourse to ECCB credit only through the Lombard Facility. The Lombard loans could be priced at a penalty over rates prevailing on the interbank market to help stimulate activity in the interbank market, and the Lombard rate could be used by the ECCB to signal its monetary stance.

The Statutory Minimum Savings Deposit Rate

The statutory minimum rate on saving deposits was introduced in 1984, at the inception of the ECCB, ostensibly in order to encourage private savings (and discourage financial disintermediation) by ensuring that the banking industry, then dominated by the branches of foreign banks, provide a positive real rate of return to depositors. To the extent that it induces a proliferation of small savings deposit accounts, it raises bank marginal costs, which in turn contributes to a wider spread between lending and deposit rates. Under conditions of excess liquidity, banks may also encounter difficulty earning an appropriate return on deposited funds given a shortage of viable investment opportunities. Consequently, in order to cover operating costs, banks could be compelled to offset the holding of excess reserves through an increase in the average lending rate. Depending on the underlying parameters characterizing the supply and demand of loanable funds, the statutory minimum savings rate could, therefore, lead to a further divergence between the average lending and average deposit rates. Furthermore high lending rates may give rise to an adverse selection problem that could undermine the stability of the banking system.

The ECCB's current plan is to propose that the statutory minimum savings rate be eliminated once the range of competing instruments is sufficiently broadened and an adequate degree of market-driven flexibility has taken hold in determining interest rates, as envisaged with the establishment of the RGSM and other money and capital market initiatives.

Banking System Soundness

The ECCB considers that the major institutions are sound, including the foreign (mainly Canadian and British) branch banks, the local subsidiaries of foreign-owned banks, and most domestic banks. A number of small domestic banks, however, operate precariously at very high asset to capital ratios. Since the ECCB was established in 1983, there has been just one case where it has had to intervene, namely the bailout in 1993 of the Bank of Montserrat, which failed largely because of bad management practices. All eight countries had to pass emergency legislation to enable the ECCB to intervene. The intervention took the form of the establishment of an ECCB subsidiary called Caribbean Assets and Liabilities Management Services Limited, which acquired the bank's bad assets (EC$15 million) in exchange for a promissory note. The Government of Montserrat became the bank's major shareholder. Recovery of the bad assets was proceeding relatively well until the eruptions of the volcano brought the island's economy to a halt in 1996–97. This legislation is still on the books, and the subsidiary still exists and can serve a similar function in the future should the need arise.

An independent assessment of the degree of compliance with ECCB requirements is precluded by the absence of published statistics on commercial bank performance. The only data available cover nonperforming loans and are limited. As of December 1998, the unsatisfactory assets to total assets ratio ranged from a low of 8 percent in Antigua and Barbuda to a high of 15 percent in Dominica, with the average for the ECCB area at about 12 percent—in excess of the maximum ratio of 10 percent permitted by the ECCB.[41] By September 1999, the regional average ratio had increased to 14.5 percent, primarily reflecting a break in the series caused by the inclusion of the commercial bank overdraft of the St. Kitts Sugar Manufacturing Corporation beginning in March 1999. When the ECCB began tightening enforcement of its guidelines, banks not in compliance were given time to reduce the bad loan portfolio according to schedules specified in the memorandum of understanding with the ECCB.

As the region's financial markets become more integrated both regionally and globally, greater competition is likely to raise both the entry and exit of firms (through mergers and acquisitions and the privatization and closure of weak government-owned banks), and the industry can be expected to undergo a process of restructuring. Thus, increased banking supervision could facilitate early identification of problem banks and prevent an escalation of the economic impact of bank failures.

Accordingly, in addition to the recent introduction of more stringent prudential requirements noted above, and the emergency legislation introduced in 1993, the ECCB has proposed a number of amendments to its charter and to the Uniform Banking Act that together would enhance prudential standards, strengthen the ECCB's hand in ensuring compliance, and allow it to act quickly should a major bank be in trouble. One is an amendment to the Charter that would give the Monetary Council circumscribed legislative powers during a bank crisis. The specifics, however, are still to be defined. Another is an amendment to the Banking Act that would enhance the ECCB's enforcement and penalization powers over financial institutions, partly through granting of authorization to issue cease and desist orders outside of the context of a banking crisis. Other proposed legislative changes include amendments to the individual acts governing offshore institutions in the member countries to make them consistent with Article 41 of the ECCB's charter, which gives it the power, effected through the Monetary Council, to regulate the licensing and monitor the operations of offshore financial institutions; harmonization of the large exposure clause in the UBA and the prudential guidelines (see above); an amendment to the UBA to allow the ECCB to execute formal memorandums of understanding with the home offices of foreign branch banks regarding supervision of the branches; an amendment to empower the ECCB to introduce additional prudential regulations; and making explicit the terms of its provision as a lender of last resort to the commercial banks.

There is also an ongoing effort to alleviate some of the legal impediments faced by banks seeking to make claims in the judicial system, which is often backlogged. A joint initiative (of the ECCB, the World Bank, the OECS Secretariat, the Caribbean Law Institute, and the U.S. AID) is under way to introduce, in each territory, alternative dispute regulation mechanisms, such as local judicial review agencies to expedite the recovery of delinquent assets.

External Policy

The key elements of the trade policy agenda are advancing trade liberalization and promoting competitiveness and export diversification. Governments face the challenge of curtailing remaining nontariff barriers and completing agreed reductions in the maximum tariff rates under the common external tariff of CARICOM. All countries but Antigua and Barbuda implemented the second stage, reducing the CET to 30 percent during 1995–97, but by early

---

[41]Unsatisfactory assets is synonymous with nonperforming assets.

> **Box 8. Stabex Grants to the Windward Islands**
>
> The European Union (EU) has been providing grants to the Windward Island countries (Dominica, Grenada, St. Lucia, and St. Vincent and the Grenadines) since the late 1980s to compensate for losses in banana export earnings (also nutmeg and cocoa in the case of Grenada) from bad weather and adverse market conditions. For each year in which there are export losses, the EU sets a Stabex allocation for each affected country and subsequently negotiates its uses with the authorities. Thus, allocations usually become available with a lag of two to three years and actual drawdowns depend on project implementation. For the Windward Islands, these Stabex allocations have become an important source of assistance amounting to ECU 169.7 million for the eight allocation years 1990–97. Of this total allocation Dominica has been assigned ECU 37.1 million, Grenada ECU 15.6 million, St. Lucia ECU 57.1 million, and St. Vincent and the Grenadines ECU 59.9 million.
>
> Stabex grants had been used mainly to support the banana industry until the EU and the authorities of the different countries concluded the Framework of Mutual Obligations (FMO) governing the use of the 1995 Stabex allocation. The FMOs had two main features: (i) the introduction of macroeconomic conditionality for the disbursement of the funds; and (ii) a marked increase in the share of Stabex resources allocated to human resource development, economic diversification, and poverty alleviation.
>
> In 1998 the EU and the authorities advanced the negotiations on the FMOs governing the use of the 1996 and 1997 Stabex allocations. The agreements for 1996–97 amounted to ECU 38 million to be disbursed in three annual tranches beginning in 1999. The release of each of the tranches was linked to meeting targets on public sector saving, on agreed levels of expenditure on health and education (consistent with the countries' public sector investment program), as well as on satisfactory implementation of the projects financed by previously released tranches. The agreements for Dominica, Grenada, and St. Lucia also envisage progress on the implementation of the common external tariff under the CARICOM Agreement.

1999 only Dominica, Grenada, and St. Vincent and the Grenadines had carried out the third stage (originally planned for implementation in the first half of 1997) that lowered the maximum tariff to 25 percent. By the same date only St. Vincent and the Grenadines had implemented the last stage of the agreement reducing the CET to 20 percent (originally planned for implementation in the first half of 1998). Grenada and St. Lucia implemented the last stage in January 2000.

The ECCB has continued to take steps to liberalize exchange controls applied to capital and nontrade current transactions. The indicative limit on foreign exchange purchases was increased in October 1997 to EC$250,000 per person per year, from EC$100,000. Purchases of foreign exchange in amounts above this limit require approval from the finance ministries, but all bona fide requests are routinely approved. The ECCB intends to continue the gradual phasing out of exchange controls.[42]

Efforts are under way to enhance the competitiveness of the banana industry. In preparation for the changes to the EU banana regime expected to take place in 2000, and with the technical and financial assistance of the EU (see Box 8), the Windward Islands started the implementation of a three-year banana recovery plan in 1998. The cornerstone of the plan is a new pricing policy involving a premium for higher quality fruit and a guaranteed price to farmers. The consensus view among stakeholders was that production had decreased largely because of reduced grower confidence in the future of the industry and inadequate prices to the grower for premium quality fruit. The average cost of production had been estimated at 30–68 EC cents per pound, depending on the farmer's efficiency (see Table 17). It was assumed that prices in the range of 36–48 EC cents would provide an incentive to most farmers to increase production to levels that would cut the cost of dead freight to a minimum, increase the price that the associations receive for the fruit, and allow them to keep the price to farmers within that range without an increase in the associations' debts (see Table 18).

In the longer term, increased emphasis is to be placed upon drainage and irrigation, with up to 2,270 acres to be supplied with drainage and 4,700 acres to be brought under irrigation over the three-year plan. Other elements of the plan include a publicity campaign to improve the profile of the sector and to encourage reinvestment, the restructuring of both local and external industry debts and enhanced extension services to improve farm management capacity. The plan is dependent upon financial commitments from the donors, the marketing and shipping joint venture of WIBDECO/FYFFES, and the banana growers associations. Partly due to this plan and to the initiatives taken earlier to improve irrigation and product quality, banana production and exports showed some pickup in 1998.

---

[42]Remaining restrictions are listed in Table 8.

V MAIN REGIONAL POLICY ISSUES

National authorities in the region think that to promote economic diversification it is essential to improve infrastructure and education, and to control costs. For this purpose, priority is given to those projects in the public sector investment program geared to improving the infrastructure for tourism and basic and vocational education. Success in diversification requires wage restraint in the public sector to avoid sparking demands for higher wages in the private sector, and maintaining a liberal policy regarding inflows of foreign labor. There is also awareness that regulatory policies need to be strengthened to avoid the cross subsidization of residential users of water and electricity by commercial users, and to bring the cost of international telecommunications and of handling cargo through the ports in certain countries to competitive levels. In this connection, it is encouraging that the sole provider of telecommunications services in the region has agreed to negotiations to revise its arrangements.[43]

---

[43]The efforts of regional governments in this area are being supported by the World Bank's OECS Telecommunications Reform Project. Its objective is to help enhance competition in the telecommunications sector and increase supply of informatics-related skills in OECS countries. The Eastern Caribbean Telecommunications Authority was established in May 2000, with the aim of harmonizing the regulatory framework for the sector.

VI Conclusions

Throughout the past 25 years of turbulence in the international financial system, the countries in the eastern Caribbean have enjoyed remarkable monetary stability. Indeed, the Eastern Caribbean Currency Union and its flagship, the ECCB, provide an impressive example of successful, long-standing monetary cooperation. The monetary and exchange arrangements maintained by the ECCB have served the region well, fostering confidence through stable domestic prices anchored in a peg to the U.S. dollar. The "strong Eastern Caribbean dollar" policy pursued by the ECCB has imposed hard limits on its ability to extend credit to participating governments. As a result, a premium has been placed on fiscal discipline, with most participating governments following prudent fiscal policies.

Price and exchange rate stability has also contributed to financial system stability. Despite the relatively frequent occurrence of major natural disasters and the secular decline of key economic activities, the financial systems in the region have remained stable and virtually free from banking crises. However, it is important that the ratio of nonperforming to total bank loans be brought down to well below the prudential guideline of 10 percent. It is encouraging, therefore, that the ECCB and member governments continue to work to safeguard financial soundness by enhancing prudential standards and extending them to nonbank financial institutions as well as offshore banks, and by strengthening compliance and intervention mechanisms.

Preserving fiscal discipline should help countries in the region maintain the value of the currency in the face of the possible phasing out of trade preferences for key exports. To support the transition to more service-based economic structures, governments in the region are seeking to improve physical and human infrastructure. To help fund such increases in public sector investment, and thereby the prospects for sustained growth, member governments should act to counter the weakening of public sector saving that has been evident in the last several years. The ECCB's fiscal reform program is a good start, but the saving targets may not be ambitious enough for some countries, especially those faced with the need to ensure the competitiveness of their banana production under a revamped EU banana regime.

Expenditure restraint, in particular containment of the government wage bill, is key to maintaining the region's competitiveness and safeguarding the currency arrangement. The latter will also require efforts to improve the flexibility of goods and factor markets, and intensified efforts at trade and capital liberalization. It is encouraging that the Monetary Council has recommended that each country establish a tripartite council on prices, wages, employment, and productivity, in recognition of the need for price and wage discipline.

The ECCB has taken the lead in efforts to extend the success of monetary cooperation to the integration of national money and capital markets. Moving from the current segmentation of financial systems to the eventual formation of a single, regional, financial space could help provide the basis for a future economic union. Achieving the latter, however, will also require substantial deepening of the links among the member countries, including through greater integration of labor and product markets. Progress toward economic integration among the Eastern Caribbean states will have to be coordinated with the formation of the single market economy, to which all CARICOM states, except the Bahamas, have formally committed themselves.

OCCASIONAL PAPERS

Recent Occasional Papers of the International Monetary Fund

195. The Eastern Caribbean Currency Union—Institutions, Performance, and Policy Issues, by Frits van Beek, José Roberto Rosales, Mayra Zermeño, Ruby Randall, and Jorge Shepherd. 2000.

194. Fiscal and Macroeconomic Impact of Privatization, by Jeffrey Davis, Rolando Ossowski, Thomas Richardson, and Steven Barnett. 2000.

193. Exchange Rate Regimes in an Increasingly Integrated World Economy, by Michael Mussa, Paul Masson, Alexander Swoboda, Esteban Jadresic, Paolo Mauro, and Andy Berg. 2000.

192. Macroprudential Indicators of Financial System Soundness, by a staff team led by Owen Evans, Alfredo M. Leone, Mahinder Gill, and Paul Hilbers. 2000.

191. Social Issues in IMF-Supported Programs, by Sanjeev Gupta, Louis Dicks-Mireaux, Ritha Khemani, Calvin McDonald, and Marijn Verhoeven. 2000.

190. Capital Controls: Country Experiences with Their Use and Liberalization, by Akira Ariyoshi, Karl Habermeier, Bernard Laurens, Inci Ötker-Robe, Jorge Iván Canales Kriljenko, and Andrei Kirilenko. 2000.

189. Current Account and External Sustainability in the Baltics, Russia, and Other Countries of the Former Soviet Union, by Donal McGettigan. 2000.

188. Financial Sector Crisis and Restructuring: Lessons from Asia, by Carl-Johan Lindgren, Tomás J.T. Baliño, Charles Enoch, Anne-Marie Gulde, Marc Quintyn, and Leslie Teo. 1999.

187. Philippines: Toward Sustainable and Rapid Growth, Recent Developments and the Agenda Ahead, by Markus Rodlauer, Prakash Loungani, Vivek Arora, Charalambos Christofides, Enrique G. De la Piedra, Piyabha Kongsamut, Kristina Kostial, Victoria Summers, and Athanasios Vamvakidis. 2000.

186. Anticipating Balance of Payments Crises: The Role of Early Warning Systems, by Andrew Berg, Eduardo Borensztein, Gian Maria Milesi-Ferretti, and Catherine Pattillo. 1999.

185. Oman Beyond the Oil Horizon: Policies Toward Sustainable Growth, edited by Ahsan Mansur and Volker Treichel. 1999.

184. Growth Experience in Transition Countries, 1990–98, by Oleh Havrylyshyn, Thomas Wolf, Julian Berengaut, Marta Castello-Branco, Ron van Rooden, and Valerie Mercer-Blackman. 1999.

183. Economic Reforms in Kazakhstan, Kyrgyz Republic, Tajikistan, Turkmenistan, and Uzbekistan, by Emine Gürgen, Harry Snoek, Jon Craig, Jimmy McHugh, Ivailo Izvorski, and Ron van Rooden. 1999.

182. Tax Reform in the Baltics, Russia, and Other Countries of the Former Soviet Union, by a Staff Team Led by Liam Ebrill and Oleh Havrylyshyn. 1999.

181. The Netherlands: Transforming a Market Economy, by C. Maxwell Watson, Bas B. Bakker, Jan Kees Martijn, and Ioannis Halikias. 1999.

180. Revenue Implications of Trade Liberalization, by Liam Ebrill, Janet Stotsky, and Reint Gropp. 1999.

179. Dinsinflation in Transition: 1993–97, by Carlo Cottarelli and Peter Doyle. 1999.

178. IMF-Supported Programs in Indonesia, Korea, and Thailand: A Preliminary Assessment, by Timothy Lane, Atish Ghosh, Javier Hamann, Steven Phillips, Marianne Schulze-Ghattas, and Tsidi Tsikata. 1999.

177. Perspectives on Regional Unemployment in Europe, by Paolo Mauro, Eswar Prasad, and Antonio Spilimbergo. 1999.

176. Back to the Future: Postwar Reconstruction and Stabilization in Lebanon, edited by Sena Eken and Thomas Helbling. 1999.

175. Macroeconomic Developments in the Baltics, Russia, and Other Countries of the Former Soviet Union, 1992–97, by Luis M. Valdivieso. 1998.

174. Impact of EMU on Selected Non–European Union Countries, by R. Feldman, K. Nashashibi, R. Nord, P. Allum, D. Desruelle, K. Enders, R. Kahn, and H. Temprano-Arroyo. 1998.

173. The Baltic Countries: From Economic Stabilization to EU Accession, by Julian Berengaut, Augusto Lopez-Claros, Françoise Le Gall, Dennis Jones, Richard Stern, Ann-Margret Westin, Effie Psalida, Pietro Garibaldi. 1998.

Occasional Papers

172. Capital Account Liberalization: Theoretical and Practical Aspects, by a staff team led by Barry Eichengreen and Michael Mussa, with Giovanni Dell'Ariccia, Enrica Detragiache, Gian Maria Milesi-Ferretti, and Andrew Tweedie. 1998.
171. Monetary Policy in Dollarized Economies, by Tomás Baliño, Adam Bennett, and Eduardo Borensztein. 1998.
170. The West African Economic and Monetary Union: Recent Developments and Policy Issues, by a staff team led by Ernesto Hernández-Catá and comprising Christian A. François, Paul Masson, Pascal Bouvier, Patrick Peroz, Dominique Desruelle, and Athanasios Vamvakidis. 1998.
169. Financial Sector Development in Sub-Saharan African Countries, by Hassanali Mehran, Piero Ugolini, Jean Phillipe Briffaux, George Iden, Tonny Lybek, Stephen Swaray, and Peter Hayward. 1998.
168. Exit Strategies: Policy Options for Countries Seeking Greater Exchange Rate Flexibility, by a staff team led by Barry Eichengreen and Paul Masson with Hugh Bredenkamp, Barry Johnston, Javier Hamann, Esteban Jadresic, and Inci Ötker. 1998.
167. Exchange Rate Assessment: Extensions of the Macroeconomic Balance Approach, edited by Peter Isard and Hamid Faruqee. 1998
166. Hedge Funds and Financial Market Dynamics, by a staff team led by Barry Eichengreen and Donald Mathieson with Bankim Chadha, Anne Jansen, Laura Kodres, and Sunil Sharma. 1998.
165. Algeria: Stabilization and Transition to the Market, by Karim Nashashibi, Patricia Alonso-Gamo, Stefania Bazzoni, Alain Féler, Nicole Laframboise, and Sebastian Paris Horvitz. 1998.
164. MULTIMOD Mark III: The Core Dynamic and Steady-State Model, by Douglas Laxton, Peter Isard, Hamid Faruqee, Eswar Prasad, and Bart Turtelboom. 1998.
163. Egypt: Beyond Stabilization, Toward a Dynamic Market Economy, by a staff team led by Howard Handy. 1998.
162. Fiscal Policy Rules, by George Kopits and Steven Symansky. 1998.
161. The Nordic Banking Crises: Pitfalls in Financial Liberalization? by Burkhard Dress and Ceyla Pazarbaşıoğlu. 1998.
160. Fiscal Reform in Low-Income Countries: Experience Under IMF-Supported Programs, by a staff team led by George T. Abed and comprising Liam Ebrill, Sanjeev Gupta, Benedict Clements, Ronald McMorran, Anthony Pellechio, Jerald Schiff, and Marijn Verhoeven. 1998.
159. Hungary: Economic Policies for Sustainable Growth, Carlo Cottarelli, Thomas Krueger, Reza Moghadam, Perry Perone, Edgardo Ruggiero, and Rachel van Elkan. 1998.
158. Transparency in Government Operations, by George Kopits and Jon Craig. 1998.
157. Central Bank Reforms in the Baltics, Russia, and the Other Countries of the Former Soviet Union, by a staff team led by Malcolm Knight and comprising Susana Almuiña, John Dalton, Inci Otker, Ceyla Pazarbaşıoğlu, Arne B. Petersen, Peter Quirk, Nicholas M. Roberts, Gabriel Sensenbrenner, and Jan Willem van der Vossen. 1997.
156. The ESAF at Ten Years: Economic Adjustment and Reform in Low-Income Countries, by the staff of the International Monetary Fund. 1997.
155. Fiscal Policy Issues During the Transition in Russia, by Augusto Lopez-Claros and Sergei V. Alexashenko. 1998.
154. Credibility Without Rules? Monetary Frameworks in the Post–Bretton Woods Era, by Carlo Cottarelli and Curzio Giannini. 1997.
153. Pension Regimes and Saving, by G.A. Mackenzie, Philip Gerson, and Alfredo Cuevas. 1997.
152. Hong Kong, China: Growth, Structural Change, and Economic Stability During the Transition, by John Dodsworth and Dubravko Mihaljek. 1997.
151. Currency Board Arrangements: Issues and Experiences, by a staff team led by Tomás J.T. Baliño and Charles Enoch. 1997.

Note: For information on the title and availability of Occasional Papers not listed, please consult the IMF Publications Catalog or contact IMF Publication Services.